# SUCCESS OR FAILURE? _____

# SUCCESS OR FAILURE? _____

*Family Planning Programs in the Third World*

DONALD J. HERNANDEZ

Foreword by Robert F. Boruch

STUDIES IN POPULATION AND URBAN DEMOGRAPHY,
NUMBER 4

Greenwood Press
Westport, Connecticut · London, England

**Library of Congress Cataloging in Publication Data**

Hernandez, Donald J.
  Success or failure?

  (Studies in population and urban demography, ISSN
0147–1104 ; no. 4)
  Bibliography: p.
  Includes index.
  1. Birth control—Developing countries.  I. Title.
II. Series.
HQ766.5.D44H47   1984      363.9′6′091716      84-6653
ISBN 0-313-24401-4 (lib. bdg.)

Library of Congress Catalog Card Number: 84-6653
ISBN: 0-313-24401-4
ISSN: 0147-1104

First published in 1984

Greenwood Press
A division of Congressional Information Service, Inc.
88 Post Road West, Westport, Connecticut 06881

Printed in the United States of America

10 9 8 7 6 5 4 3 2 1

**Copyright Acknowledgments**

  The author and publisher are grateful for permission to reprint from the following
sources.
  Donald J. Hernandez, "The Impact of Family Planning Programs on Fertility in Developing Countries: A Critical Evaluation," *Social Science Research* 10 (1981):32–66.
  Donald J. Hernandez, "A Note on Measuring the Independent Impact of Family
Planning Programs on Fertility Declines," *Demography* 18, no. 4 (November 1981):627–
634.

To Frank and Marguerite

# Contents

viii    Contents

# Illustrations

# Tables

# Foreword

Governments and private foundations have not always been attentive to evidence about what works. The exceptions are remarkable, and some admirable exceptions lie in research on fertility control programs. At least some of the exceptions are given in a fine catalog of fertility control project evaluations compiled by Cuca and Pierce (1977) for the World Bank. For example, randomized field experiments are very desirable on scientific grounds because when conducted properly they produce fair and unbiased estimates of the program's effect. Yet controlled, randomized experiments constitute a minority of evaluations that Cuca and Pierce list so conscientiously. Doubtless they are a minority because they demand considerable extra-scientific skill—managerial, bureaucratic, and political expertise—that is often unavailable.

As Hernandez observes, attention to quality of evidence has, however, increased in recent years. The origins of the stress lie partly with conscientious bureaucrats and scholars who are able to reiterate the need to take data seriously, to assure such data are collected, and to produce incentives for doing so. Those efforts are virtuous, especially in view of their infrequency, and they are exhibited from time to time in projects supported by UNESCO, the World Bank, the U.S. Agency for International Development, the Ford Foundation, and especially by the Population Council.

The importance of fertility control itself is clear from high average birth rates of women in countries such as Kenya, where the average woman has eight children, and from evidence that increases in health services may actually increase birth rates in Syria, Bangladesh, Bolivia, and elsewhere. The rate has a substantial impact on a country's efforts to enhance the well-being of its population, on some local and regional development programs, and on individuals themselves.

The importance of the problem of determining what works is also clear in principle. We need to understand whether and why our ef-

forts succeed or fail in order to do better. The business of developing
fair estimates of program effects is complicated at best in that resources for data collection and quality control of data are scarce, the
matter of data collection is treated with indifference, incompetence, or
corruption, and the designs for field research are often such that no
unambiguous evidence is produceable. Moreover, as Hernandez emphasizes here, disentangling effects of various kinds of demographic
changes from changes produced by fertility control programs requires
considerable expertise, if indeed the research design makes this possible at all.

No field research is perfect, of course: even marvelous exceptions
contain some flaws. The exceptions are valuable nonetheless. Hernandez pushes the available evidence at the country level to its limits to
understand what can and cannot be said about the effectiveness of
fertility control programs and projects. In doing so, he conscientiously
and benignly capitalizes on a systematic approach to enumerating the
strengths and weaknesses of studies, selecting the ones that are sus-
ceptible to the fewest severe threats to validity, and educing implications about program impact.

Hernandez's approach is analytic and directs attention to country
level rather than project level data. Other approaches are no less important. For example, learning how to better manage large-scale controlled experiments that yield less equivocal, less biased estimates of
program effects and help the conscientious manager to improve programs is crucial to advances in this arena. Hernandez takes pains, for
instance, to recognize some of the work that pertains to resolving
managerial, political-institutional, and ethical problems that are en-
gendered by sophisticated pilot tests of programs, including experiments and demonstration projects.

Hernandez adds to what we understand about the nature of fertility control issues and the evidence bearing on purported solutions. More
important, this treatise is a guide to how information on the effectiveness of programs should be obtained. Some of the guidance is implicit
and understated—randomized field experiments on pilot versions of
programs are difficult to mount but essential, for instance. But we must,
in parallel, learn more about how to analyze less perfect approaches.
We must generate, as Hernandez does, alternative estimates of program effect, when this is appropriate, and learn how to appraise and
use them. We are unlikely to discover more effective ways to do what
seems to be sensible until we learn to conduct more systematic experiments and to account for the competing explanations in the more easily
managed quasi-experimental approaches to understanding.

## REFERENCE

Cuca, R., and C. S. Pierce. 1977. Experiments in family planning: Lessons from the developing world. Baltimore: The Johns Hopkins University Press for the World Bank.

Robert F. Boruch

# Acknowledgments

This monograph is the product of an extended research effort. I am particularly indebted to Judith Blake for suggesting that I pursue this line of inquiry and for generously providing invaluable reactions to earlier drafts of the work included here. I am also greatly indebted to Kingsley Davis for his invariably thoughtful and thought-provoking ideas and to Prithwis Das Gupta for his mathematical and methodological insights. To all three I wish to express my appreciation for the enthusiastic encouragement which they offered throughout the preparation of this monograph.

The arguments, analyses, and conclusions presented here also benefited substantially from the comments and suggestions provided by many other scholars. For their willing help, I am grateful to Beth Berkov, Joseph A. Cavanaugh, Harvey Choldin, David Heer, David E. Myers, Jorge Del Pinal, Robert Parke, Jeanne Clare Ridley, Eui-Hang Shin, David L. Sills, Glenna D. Spitze, Stewart E. Tolnay, Murray Webster, Leila Rosen Young, and several anonymous reviewers.

I would also like to thank Marian Anderson, Jan Reedstrom, and Judith Sornberger for editorial assistance, Eunice Y. Bakanic, Tammy Chen, Kenneth Cockrell, Virginia Hood, and Pi-Hsia Kao for research assistance, and Karen Crouse, Martha George, Suzanne Glover, Marilyn Haworth, and Pamela Nall for tireless typing.

Financial support in the preparation of this monograph was gratefully received from the National Institutes of Health and the Department of Demography at the University of California, Berkeley through a graduate traineeship, from the University of South Carolina through research leave, and from the National Science Foundation under Grant SOC 7721686. Of course, the views expressed here are not necessarily shared by the scholars who kindly read earlier drafts or by the institutions which provided financial support.

Portions of Chapters 1 and 2 were published previously, in a slightly different form, in *Social Science Research*, and portions of Chapters 8 and 9 are drawn from an article published in *Demography*. My thanks are due to these journals for permission to republish this material.

Finally, I would especially like to express my deep appreciation to Lyla, my wife, for cheerful and unstinting help, advice, and encouragement.

# SUCCESS
# OR
# FAILURE? _____

# 1

# The Programs and the Controversy

The population of the third world expanded dramatically during the last two decades, by a magnitude unprecedented in human history, as it grew from 2.1 billion people in 1960 to 3.3 billion in 1980 (United Nations, 1981). This multiplication of humanity is alarming to many national and international leaders and others, because they view it as a major force contributing to the extreme poverty and deprivation in many third world countries. As a means of slowing this growth, public policies to reduce aggregate fertility levels have been advocated. The most widely implemented fertility reduction policy has been family planning programs that distribute modern birth control technology to individuals and couples who desire to limit their own fertility. The purpose of this monograph is to determine whether these family planning programs have been a success or a failure as an independent policy initiative in reducing fertility and hence population growth in the third world.

The effectiveness of family planning programs as an independent policy initiative has been seriously questioned within the social science community, but the debate surrounding the success or the failure of these programs is of more than purely scientific interest, because its resolution has critical implications for the welfare of billions of people and for an array of national and international policies. This introductory chapter presents the context for and major issues involved in this controversy by discussing the predominance of family planning programs as the policy adopted in most third world countries that seek to reduce fertility, additional fertility reduction policies that have been recommended or have been implemented in a few key third world countries, and the ideas underpinning the scientific debate regarding the success or the failure of family planning programs.

## PREDOMINANCE OF FAMILY PLANNING PROGRAMS

The United Nations Declaration on Population signed by 30 heads of state during 1966 and 1967 asserts:

We believe that the population problem must be recognized as a principal element in long-range national planning if governments are to achieve their economic goals and fulfill the aspirations of their people.

We believe that the great majority of parents desire to have the knowledge and the means to plan their families; that the opportunity to decide the number and spacing of children is a basic human right (Studies in Family Planning, 1967:1; 1968:3).

Reinforcing the United Nations Declaration, formal philosophical inquiries into the ethical status of alternative fertility reduction policies have argued with virtual unanimity that voluntary family planning programs are the most ethically preferable of the policies evaluated, because they enhance freedom and justice by providing knowledge and technology that allow individuals to make and implement more fully informed personal decisions about the number and spacing of their children (Hernandez, 1984).

Congruent with these declarations, Nortman (1982) reports for 134 third world countries in 1982 that 72 of them officially support family planning programs, more than half (39) with the aim of reducing their population growth rate. More important, 94 percent of the people in the third world live in countries that officially support family planning programs, and 78 percent live in countries that explicitly seek to reduce population growth by supporting these programs (Nortman, 1982). Whether the ultimate goals of family planning policies relate to population growth, human rights, health, or something else, nearly all family planning programs in third world countries seek most immediately to insure access to modern birth control technology by distributing supplies, providing services, and offering information about these supplies and services to individuals and couples who desire to limit their own fertility.

Expenditures in the third world for these activities now exceed $1 billion (U.S.) annually (Lewison, 1983). An estimated $100 million is spent by individuals to obtain supplies and services, over $400 million is spent by third world governments on their own programs, and about $450 million is provided by governments and private agencies in developed countries. The U.S. Agency for International Development is the largest single donor, and in 1981 all U.S. donors accounted for about 50 percent of the family planning program aid from developed countries to third world countries. The level of aid from the United States reflects not only its continuing commitment but also its early and critical role in encouraging the implementation of family planning programs throughout the third world. Of the 12 principal donor countries, the remaining 11 from largest to smallest contributor are Japan, Sweden, Norway, West Germany, the United Kingdom, the Netherlands, Canada, Denmark, Australia, Switzerland, and Belgium.

Recent results from the World Fertility Survey (Lightbourne and Singh, 1982) provide statistical indicators which at least suggest that family planning programs may have been relatively successful in many third world countries in achieving their immediate goal—the provision of supplies, services, and information about modern birth control methods to individual women and couples. For example, among 29 third world countries, the survey found that in 25 of them more than 75 percent of all currently married, fecund women know about such methods. And among 30 third world countries, the survey found for currently married, fecund women that, although the percentage currently using contraception is less than 20 percent in seven countries, the percentage is 20–39 percent in 12 countries, 40–59 percent in 10 countries, and 71 percent in one country. For purposes of comparison it can be noted that in 13 of 16 developed countries (European plus the United States) the corresponding figures exceed 60 percent. Hence, contraceptive usage rates in many third world countries are substantial but typically remain well below the rates for developed countries.

Although these indicators, pertaining to the immediate goal of family planning programs, appear to suggest considerable success, the indicators that are most critical for present purposes are fertility and ultimately population growth. In the third world as a whole, between the period 1960 to 1965 and the period 1975 to 1980 the Crude Birth Rate (CBR) and Gross Reproduction Rate (GRR) both declined by about 20 percent, but as noted earlier the population of the third world expanded during this period from 2.1 billion people to 3.3 billion. Looking to the future, assuming further declines of about 20 percent in the CBR and about 30 percent in the GRR between the period 1975 to 1980 and the period 1995 to 2000, the U.N. medium projection suggests that the population of the third world will expand by an additional 1.5 billion to reach 4.8 billion in the year 2000.

These statistics prompt the question: Will family planning programs produce fertility declines of the magnitude required to bring population growth to a level that is consistent with an alleviation of poverty and deprivation and an improvement in human welfare in third world countries? Although these population projections may suggest to many observers that additional fertility reduction policies appear necessary in the future, the prior question is whether, or to what extent, family planning programs are responsible, as an independent initiative, for past fertility declines. If factors other than family planning programs are responsible for past declines, then future declines also may depend upon other factors and/or upon the introduction of additional fertility reduction policies. What form might such policies take? Because of the possible need for additional fertility reduction policies, this question merits brief consideration before turning to the principal concern of the present monograph, namely, how successful family planning programs have been in the past.

## ADDITIONAL FERTILITY REDUCTION PROGRAMS

Singapore and China already have judged that national fertility declines in the absence of additional policies were unlikely to be substantial enough, and have implemented programs relying upon incentives, disincentives, and political pressures of various types. Indonesia also has implemented a program that appears to incorporate political pressures not found in typical family planning programs, and it is experimenting with community incentives. Regarding potential fertility reduction policies, the World Population Plan of Action of the United Nations (1979a) recommends that countries wishing to affect fertility levels give priority to implementing socioeconomic development programs which will have a decisive impact on fertility, and various scholars have recommended a variety of socioeconomic and community incentive programs.

Singapore began in 1968 to augment its family planning program by instituting incentives and disincentives directed toward individuals and couples to encourage small family sizes.[1] Then with a dramatic halt during 1970–72 in the prior fertility decline, the government announced additional policy measures concerned with hospital delivery fees, maternity leave, education, income taxes, and housing (Anderson, Cheng, and Wan, 1977; Saw, 1980; Fawcett and Khoo, 1980).

Delivery fees in government hospitals, where more than 80 percent of all births take place, are calculated now on a sliding scale to increase with higher birth orders. Maternity leave is granted only for the first and second births. Priority in primary school placements is given to children of the first or second birth order. Income tax deductions for children are calculated on a sliding scale to decrease at higher birth orders, with no deduction allowed for a fourth or subsequent child born on or after August 1, 1973. Government housing, where 60 percent of the population lived in 1977, is no longer restricted to families with five or more members, and only families with three or fewer children are allowed to sublet rooms.

Additional incentives and disincentives also have been implemented, and restrictions on sterilization and abortion were eliminated during this period. And numerous conditions within the society also appear to have facilitated and encouraged fertility declines, including a relatively weak traditional family organization, a relatively strong and well-respected government, rapid social and economic development, and an upward striving and achievement orientation (Fawcett and Khoo, 1980).

Indonesia is the fifth most populous country in the world, exceeded only by China and India among third world countries. With the aim of slowing population growth, Indonesia has supplemented a family planning program approach, especially in Bali and East Java, with an administrative strategy that harnesses the authority of local community structures to persuade, if not coerce, couples to limit their fertility (Hull, Hull, and Singarimbun, 1977; McNicoll, 1980; Jacobsen, 1983).[2]

The central government has directed public servants and the military to promote the family planning program in every way, and it issues directives which are transmitted through lower levels of government to individual hamlets. As a means of encouraging the attainment of contraceptive acceptor targets, the current contraceptive behavior of couples is closely monitored by the local community through the public display of color-coded community maps, and contraceptive behavior is reviewed publicly at monthly community meetings. In some areas the local leader bangs a drum daily to remind women to take their birth control pills. In short, to reinforce family planning program efforts that are designed to insure the availability of birth control technology, the central government utilizes networks of communication and loyalty to mobilize peer pressure that encourages and prompts couples to adopt contraception. More recently, Indonesia also initiated a community incentive program in which nearly 60 villages where at least 35 percent of the couples practice contraception will receive additional financial support for community projects such as roads or income-generating activities.

With a population of more than 1 billion people, China is pursuing a fertility reduction policy that is more ambitious, comprehensive, and stringent than any other in the world (Chen and Kols, 1982; Aird, 1982; Jacobsen, 1983; Tien, 1983).[3] China has initiated a one-child-per-couple policy, because it views the achievement of zero population growth by the year 2000 as essential for the success of the four modernizations of agriculture, industry, defense, and technology and science. More specifically, the one-child norm was adopted during 1979 because of the perception that an expected increase of 50 percent in the number of women reaching marriage age and the reproductive years would lead, even if these women were to bear an average of no more than two children, to population growth that would severely hamper the nation's ability to feed, clothe, and shelter its people. The current one-child campaign relies upon a wide array of incentives and disincentives, and upon politically organized social pressure and compulsion.

The central government of China is responsible for funding and insuring the availability of contraceptive supplies and surgical services, while local communities are responsible for paying the wages of local birth planning personnel and for implementing specific incentives and disincentives. Although particular incentives and penalties vary somewhat across communities, they broadly encompass income, housing, health, old age, children's education, and children's jobs. Couples who agree to limit themselves to one child may receive a monthly stipend (in urban areas) or extra work points (in rural areas) equal to 5 to 8 percent of average income until the child reaches age 14. And in rural areas they also may receive an adult's ration of food for the child, and the child may count for 1.5 or 2 persons in the allocation of private farming plots. The couple may be allocated living space similar in size to that of a two-child family, and in urban areas preferential access to public housing. They may receive an extra two weeks of paid maternity leave, and special access to health care for the child. The couple may be guaranteed special pension benefits. And the child may receive highest priority for admission to school, exemption from tuition fees, and highest priority in receiving a desirable job assignment upon reaching working age.

Parents who exceed the one-child norm, in contrast, are penalized. For example, they may be required to return all the stipends or work points formerly received as a benefit under the one-child policy. They also may be required to pay for each extra child's food ration, or be fined an average annual income, or be subject to a 10 percent reduction in annual income or work points, or have previously assigned private farming plots taken away, or be defined as ineligible for three years for promotions, pay increases, etc.

These incentives and disincentives are embedded within an administrative system of central political control and strong community organization. National reproductive norms are established and translated into targets for local groups, and leaders at all levels are held responsible for insuring compliance with these targets. At the local level, birth planning groups assign permission to only certain couples to bear children during a specific time period. These decisions are implemented through group study sessions and through direct and personal social pressure. Although education, persuasion, and voluntarism are stressed, harassment and coercion have been reported, as women are "mobilized" to have IUDs inserted, or to have unauthorized pregnancies terminated, or to be sterilized (Chen and Kols, 1982; Aird, 1982; Jacobsen, 1983; Tien, 1983).

The perceived need to employ political pressure and, at times, coercive measures to compel parents to limit themselves to one child suggests that many parents have a strong desire to bear more than one child, but particularly a son, especially in rural agricultural areas. The high proportion of parents with a son among those who have agreed to limit themselves to one child (two out of three) and the prevalence of female infanticide and the neglect of females also point in the same direction (Tien, 1983). And the agricultural responsibility system adopted in 1979 may have increased the value of children to agricultural parents. As a countervailing force, additional incentives, disincentives, and efforts to equalize the status of men and women have been adopted (Chen and Kols, 1982; Tien, 1983). Furthermore, the Central Committee of the Chinese Communist Party firmly maintains, "We must popularize the practice of one child for each couple, strictly control second births, and resolutely prevent additional births" (Tien, 1983:6).

Considerably short of policies that promote fertility reductions through political pressure or coercion, the United Nations and/or various scholars have recommended that socioeconomic development policies be selected based on their likely effect on fertility, and that community incentive policies, such as the one recently initiated by Indonesia, be pursued. For example, the World Population Plan of Action (United Nations, 1979a:43) states:

It is recommended that countries wishing to affect fertility levels give priority to implementing development programmes and educational and health strategies which, while contributing to economic growth and higher standards of living, have a decisive impact upon demographic trends, including fertility. International co-operation is called for to give priority to assisting such national efforts in order that these programmes and strategies be carried into effect.

Scholars such as Blake (1965), Dixon (1978a), Cochrane (1979), and Repetto (1979) have explicitly recommended—as specific socioeconomic policies that appear likely to encourage fertility reductions—increased female labor force participation, increased education, particularly for women, and the redistribution of income. Such recommendations appear to date to have had little effect, however, on the actual selection of specific alternative policies by third world countries or by international agencies concerned with reducing fertility, although experiments linking community development efforts with birth control and fertility behavior are underway in Thailand (David, 1982).

Other scholars such as Kangas (1970) and McNicoll (1975; 1978; 1980) have recommended the implementation of community incentive policies that would take into account the critical role of the extended family and local community in the fertility behavior of individuals (Hernandez, 1984). Such policies would offer incentives to entire local communities in third world countries in return for limiting their fertility, thereby providing these communities with visible and tangible benefits, not only immediately but over the long term. These recommendations too have had little apparent impact on specific national and international fertility reduction policies, although the important initiative in Indonesia should be noted again and followed with considerable interest.

Recommendations for public policies such as these, in which fertility reduction goals are linked directly to socioeconomic initiatives or community incentives, seek to explicitly evoke consequences for fertility that socioeconomic conditions implicitly have had in the past. Hence, advocates of these policies particularly focus on critical elements in socioeconomic conditions which not only have been responsible, historically, for major sustained fertility declines but also are amenable to explicit public policy interventions that could mimic historical relationships and changes. Fertility reduction policies that rely upon socioeconomic initiatives and community incentives are promising avenues for effectively augmenting family planning programs precisely because they seek to identify and alter key elements in people's lives—such as education, work, income, and social status—which appear to have been critical in the transformation of reproductive motivation and behavior that characterized the long-term fertility declines in the developed countries during the Industrial Revolution.

The implicit but pervasive influence of socioeconomic conditions on fertility also provides the foundation for the scholarly position in the debate about the success or failure of family planning programs, which argues that family planning programs are not likely, by themselves, to bring about major reductions in fertility that are independent of causally prior socioeconomic conditions and changes. Such arguments are buttressed by the fact that the historical fertility declines in the developed countries occurred not only in the absence of government organized family planning programs but also in the face of extensive legal restrictions on the dissemination of birth control information and devices.

In view of these facts and arguments, if decisions about future fertility reduction policies in the third world are to be well-informed and successful in initiating fertility declines of the desired magnitude, then information already discussed here briefly about the range of possible policies is of obvious value. But equally important is knowledge about the effects on fertility of past socioeconomic conditions and of past fertility reduction policies, because this knowledge can suggest promising future directions for new fertility reduction policies.

## THE SCIENTIFIC DEBATE

Scholars who deny that family planning programs per se have an independent effect on fertility argue instead, from historical precedent, that socioeconomic conditions and the resulting reproductive motivation of individuals together determine the extent to which individuals limit their own fertility, and hence the extent to which national fertility levels change through time. As suggested above, socioeconomic changes associated with the inception and spread of the Industrial Revolution appear to have been responsible for the most dramatic, long-term, and widespread fertility declines that have occurred in the modern history of the world.

In offering an explanation for these fertility reductions, Davis (1963) suggests that individuals and families sought to take advantage of emerging economic opportunities, and to avoid a relative loss of social and economic status compared to others who also were taking advantage of these opportunities, by responding with changes in demographic behavior that included limiting their family size. The result was sustained declines in aggregate fertility. Blake (1973) also calls attention to how the institutional structures of societies influence the reproductive motivation, and hence the fertility, of individuals by defining the rewards and the sacrifices that are associated with bearing and rearing children.

In developing a formal conceptual model of the utilities and costs of children to their parents, Blake discusses a wide variety of economic and noneconomic factors that foster sustained declines in fertility during the socioeconomic transition from a rural-agricultural to an urban-industrial society. For example, she argues that economic costs of child rearing which are camouflaged in subsistence economies by the lack of monetized transactions become quite salient when monetized trade becomes more prevalent. She argues that when services such as formal education, medical care, and dental care become increasingly available, the perceived need to take advantage of them increases the cost of child rearing. She argues that noneconomic costs of child rearing, which are shared and hence diffused in agricultural societies where couples live in close proximity to a tightly knit kinship network, tend to increase and become a burden to parents in transitional societies where they have less easy access to relatives who will provide child care. The sheer time which parents must devote to child care may increase substantially.

Blake argues that the indirect costs of children also increase during the transition from a rural-agricultural to an urban-industrial society. With industrialization or economic development comes a proliferation of consumer goods and services which compete with children for time and money. The quantity and quality of clothing, housing, travel, and recreation that can be afforded are much greater for a couple with one or two children than for a couple with a large number of children to care for. The participation of both the husband and the wife in the labor force of a transitional society may limit the time available for child care, and the care of large numbers of children can require the sacrifice of employment outside the home by one of the parents, usually the mother. But employment in the nonagricultural sector can provide a woman with an alternative to children, or at least to a large number of children, as the sole or primary source of social status and personal satisfaction. All of these, and still other changes that occur with socioeconomic development tend to encourage individuals and couples to bear and rear fewer children, leading to long-term fertility declines.

Because social and economic conditions such as these appear, even in the face of government opposition to birth control technology, to have been responsible for the sustained fertility declines that developed countries experienced historically during the transition from a rural-agricultural society to an urban-industrial one, some social scientists have argued that major fertility declines will not occur in third world countries without such socioeconomic changes, regardless of the implementation of family planning programs that provide birth control information and services to couples.

This position holds that if in response to changing socioeconomic conditions individuals and couples must limit their fertility to achieve their reproductive goals, then they will actively seek and adopt some means of limiting births. Given strong motivation, they will identify and employ means of limiting fertility. Otherwise, contraceptive technology remains unused. The relative availability and perceived costs of different birth control methods may influence the decision of which one to adopt, but not the prior decision to limit or not limit fertility. If a family planning program is introduced, the technology it supplies is seen simply as substituting for means of fertility control that would have been employed in the absence of the program, and the underlying socioeconomic conditions are seen, consequently, as the fundamental determinant of any fertility change that occurs. Since the family planning program simply is substituting for other means of fertility control, it is conceived as not making an independent contribution to the fertility decline. In advocating this motivational view of fertility, Davis asserts:

If it were admitted that the creation and care of new human beings is so-
cially motivated, like other forms of behavior, by being a part of the system
of rewards and punishments that is built into human relationships, and thus
is bound up with the individual's economic and personal interests, it would
be apparent that the social structure and economy must be changed before a
deliberate reduction in the birth rate can be achieved (1967: 733).

Why, if the most important historical fertility declines occurred because of socioeconomic changes and in the face of legal restrictions on
birth control technology, would one expect a policy initiative directed
toward disseminating birth control information and services to have
an effect on fertility that is independent of other indigenous socioeconomic conditions and changes?[4] Ravenholt and Chao, who hold to
this technological view, assert:

Although a number of factors may influence fertility over the long run—
including education, per capita income, employment and status of women, and
availability of housing and jobs—these recent data strongly suggest that over
the short run, for developing countries today, the most important single factor in attainment of sharp fertility declines is the *availability* of more effective methods of fertility control distributed through vigorous nation-wide family
planning programs (1974a: 223; 1974b: J–22).

The position affirming that family planning programs can have an
independent effect on fertility consists of three analytically distinct
arguments. First, people who are motivated to limit their fertility, but
unable to find a means of birth control, will engender children they
do not want. A program instituted in this situation can provide birth
control technology to such people and reduce unwanted fertility. Second, if a family planning program distributes birth control technology
that is more effective than the means of fertility limitation that would
have been employed in the absence of the program, then people who
substitute the program for indigenous birth control methods will di-
minish their unwanted fertility.

Third, program efficacy extends beyond providing instrumentalities
by fostering changes in reproductive motivation which influence the
demand for birth control, the use of birth control, and fertility. Specifically, the educational and informational component of the program—including mass media campaigns, field-worker activities, pos-
ters, and so on—along with the general diffusion of information, owing
to any increased availability of contraception, could both legitimize and
influence people to adopt small family values and birth control methods, thereby reducing their fertility. This third type of program effect
is known as a spillover effect because the program's impact is seen as

spilling over to women who are not acceptors of program supplied contraception.

The divergent positions of the motivational and technological schools of thought can be summarized as two hypotheses. The *indigenous fertility decline hypothesis* of the motivational school consists of three components. First, fertility declined indigenously because any reduction in the number of children desired grew out of socioeconomic conditions and changes in them. Second, fertility declined indigenously because the demand for fertility control was supplied outside the family planning program, or would have been had the program not existed. Third, fertility declined indigenously from involuntary causes.[5]

The *net fertility decline hypothesis* of the technological school consists of two components. The family planning program produced a net fertility decline either because it supplied a demand for effective fertility control that would otherwise have been unmet, or because it generated a reduction in the desired number of children and hence the attendant fertility decline.

Although the indigenous and net decline hypotheses might each explain part of the fertility decline in a specific third world country, the contradictory conclusions of past studies, many of which were conducted or funded by the agencies involved in implementing family planning programs, have fueled controversy surrounding these hypotheses. The question of the success or failure of family planning programs can be stated less formally. Have family planning programs succeeded in generating fertility declines that are independent of the fertility declines that would have occurred in their absence because of indigenous socioeconomic conditions and ongoing socioeconomic changes? Or have family planning programs been a failure as an independent policy initiative because socioeconomic conditions and change are responsible for the fertility declines that have occurred?

The purpose of this monograph is to reconcile the conflicting claims of past studies by analyzing the validity of the research designs that they employed and by developing a series of new estimates of the net program impact that utilize the best available research designs.[6] The primary temporal focus of these analyses is on the period spanning the mid–1960s to the mid–1970s, during which family planning programs were widely adopted, but prior to the implementation of major policy efforts directed toward augmenting such programs with incentives, disincentives, and political pressures of various types. Substantively, this monograph focuses on estimating the success of family planning programs (1) in specific countries that appear to many observers to have implemented especially successful programs during this period, and (2) in the third world as a whole through cross-national analyses encompassing many third world countries.

## NOTES

1. Family planning programs are organized mainly to provide modern birth control supplies, services, and information. Although such programs also may offer small, one-time payments to acceptors, doctors, or family planning workers, these payments are not intended as inducements to acceptance and, hence, are not properly viewed as incentives (Jacobsen, 1983: 7–13). Family planning programs per se are contrasted here with more comprehensive programs that have been augmented with components that include substantial incentives, disincentives, and/or political pressure, such as the current programs of Singapore, Indonesia, and China.

2. Also see Edmondson (1981) for a study of the factors that influence both family planning program strength and fertility in Bali.

3. Also see Tien (1984) for a discussion of how the Chinese program differs from most other family planning programs in third world countries, and for a study of the effect of the Chinese policy and socioeconomic change on fertility in China.

4. Proponents of the motivational view include Davis (1963; 1967; 1971; 1972), Blake (1965; 1973), Hauser (1969), Tabarrah (1971), Mamdani (1972), and Blake and Das Gupta (1975). Among those advocating the technological view are Berelson (1963), Bogue (1967), Freedman and Takeshita (1969), Chang, Liu, and Chow (1969), Kirk (1969), Bumpass and Westoff (1970), Ravenholt and Chao (1974a; 1974b), Freedman and Berelson (1976), and Srikantan (1977).

5. See Davis and Blake (1956) for a more detailed discussion of the intermediate variables.

6. Hauser (1967; 1969), Mauldin (1968), Seltzer (1970), Reynolds (1972; 1973), Wolfers (1975), and Wells (1975) discuss various deficiencies of many of these studies. The present evaluation is more comprehensive, systematic, and detailed. In addition, the United Nations (1978; 1979b; 1982) has published three documents which raise many of the methodological concerns that are developed here, but these documents do not systematically apply these concerns to the evaluation of the relative validity of earlier studies on this topic. Although some of the research evaluated here may not have been intended to bear directly on the net fertility decline hypothesis, all the studies may be conceived as providing evidence on it, and are analyzed here as such.

# 2

# Reconciling the Contradictory Conclusions of Past Studies

## POTENTIAL THREATS TO THE VALIDITY OF PAST STUDIES

The contradictory conclusions of past studies can be reconciled by identifying and assessing the differences in their design and implementation that account for the discrepancies between the inferences they draw. The best approach to discovering the strengths and weaknesses of past studies is to compare them to the ideal research design.[1] The "true experiment," which is the exemplary scientific procedure for determining whether or not two variables are related as cause and effect, is embodied in the following research design.

First, a group of women is chosen for study, and these subjects are randomly assigned to either an experimental or a control group.[2] Second, the experimental group is exposed to the family planning program, but the control group is not. Third, after an appropriate time interval, the fertility of the two groups is measured and compared. If their fertility is the same, we infer the program had no net impact, but if the fertility of the experimental group is less than that of the control group, we infer the program produced a fertility reduction that would not have occurred in its absence. The net program effect is estimated by subtracting control group fertility from experimental group fertility.

The inference that the experimental group fertility decline was generated by the program, excluding other causes, requires the presence of a control group, because it provides the baseline for measuring the magnitude of the program effect. Random assignment of subjects to treatment groups ensures that the groups are as similar as possible with regard to motivation, knowledge, and other potentially relevant variables. Because random assignment creates experimental and control groups that have a known distribution on all nontreatment factors and their effects, these effects can be taken into account with statistical tests to estimate the independent treatment effect.[3]

This experimental design has not been implemented with fertility as the dependent variable in any study that has come to the attention of this author.[4] Quasi-experiments, which are distinguished from true experiments by the absence of random assignment of subjects to treatment groups, have been implemented instead. Because true experiments are more valid than quasi-experiments, the relative validity of various quasi-experiments can be assessed by using the true experiment as a standard of comparison.

The quasi-experimental design most similar to the true experiment is the "nonequivalent control group design," which might take the following form as a means of assessing family planning program efficacy.[5] First, a program is implemented throughout a country and several years pass. Then a group of family planning program acceptors is chosen as the experimental group, and a group of women who are not program acceptors is selected as the preliminary control group. Then a *subset* of the preliminary control group that is matched with the experimental group along specific dimensions, perhaps age and education, is chosen as the final control group. Now a pretest and posttest are conducted, that is, the fertility of both groups is measured for periods preceding and following program implementation. If the fertility decline of the experimental group is greater than that of the control group, we infer the program produced a net fertility decline, the magnitude of which is estimated as the difference between the two declines.

This quasi-experiment is similar to a true experiment except that there is no random assignment of subjects to treatment groups. This difference in treatment group selection generates four potential internal validity threats: self-selection history interaction, self-selection maturation interaction, other self-selection interactions, and statistical regression artifacts.[6]

Before discussing these threats, history and maturation, which are potential validity threats that undermine some quasi-experiments but not the nonequivalent control group design, must be described. History undermines a study if between the beginning and end of the study historical events other than the family planning program produce fertility change and if the research fails to empirically distinguish between the effects of history and the program. For example, female labor force participation reduces the fertility of working women below what it would be if they were not working. Hence, if female labor force participation increased at the same time a family planning program was instituted, the effects of this historical event and the program might be confounded. Maturation refers to the possibility that the fertility of an aggregation of people changes systematically through time.[7] If maturation is producing fertility decline, for example, and if a research design cannot distinguish between maturation and program generated decrease, then maturation is a plausible rival to the net fertility decline hypothesis.

The nonequivalent control group quasi-experiment is not plagued by these threats because it compares fertility change for an experimental and a control group, both of which are subject to history and maturation. Consequently, the comparison between the fertility changes of the two groups reflects the program impact, controlling for history and maturation. When the criteria used to select treatment groups produce or reflect differential exposure to relevant historical events and differential maturation, however, the selection procedures interact with history and maturation to produce a subtle yet serious internal validity threat. This threat undermines the nonequivalent control group quasi-experiment described above.

For instance, suppose that increasing female labor force participation and family planning program implementation occur simultaneously, and that working women experience greater fertility decline than nonworkers. Suppose further that the program has no net effect on the entire population. Now, in order to produce their sharper fertility reduction, a larger proportion of working than nonworking women must use birth control technology,[8] that is, working women will make greater use of all sources of birth control technology, including family planning program supplied technology. Consequently, the selection procedures generate an experimental group in which female workers are over-represented and a control group in which nonworkers are over-represented. In other words, the selection procedures produce an experimental group for whom historical events—entry into the labor force—produce inordinately rapid fertility decline, and they generate a control group with inordinately slow fertility decline. A comparison of the fertility reductions of the two groups will then *necessarily* show a net family planning program effect, although none actually exists. Similarly, any actual net program effect would necessarily be exaggerated because it is muddled with the selection-history interaction.

This type of reasoning is generalized easily to show that this research design necessarily confounds any net program effect with all historical events, with all maturational processes, and with all other fertility determinants that generate differential fertility change. The research design guarantees that women experiencing fertility decline from all nonprogram causes are over-represented in the experimental group and under-represented in the control group because it assigns acceptors to the experimental group and nonacceptors to the control group *after both sets of women have been given the opportunity to become acceptors*. The result of these self-selection interactions is that any independent program effect is overestimated.[9]

The severity of this problem may be reduced by creating treatment groups, composed of subsets of all acceptors and/or nonacceptors, that are matched with regard to some nonprogram fertility determinants. Although this matching equates the two groups on these particular nonprogram causes of fertility, the groups are necessarily undermatched because fertility is the lawful product of innumerable causes and any particular set of matching variables does not completely measure all these causes. Therefore, matching can mitigate, but never eliminate, the validity threats posed by self-selection interactions, and this quasi-experiment necessarily overestimates any net program impact.

Regression artifacts pose a fourth internal validity threat to this quasi-experiment, if fertility is subject to measurement error or random fluctuations, and if subjects are selected for a treatment group because of their extreme pretest fertility or because of their extreme scores on a variable correlated with fertility. If these conditions obtain, the treatment group posttest fertility predictably approaches or regresses toward the mean fertility of the larger population from which it was chosen.

For example, if the fertility of individual women is somewhat random, which it is, and if a subset of all women is chosen as the experimental group because of its high pretest fertility, then this subset tends to include women with "abnormally" high pretest fertility. Hence, on the posttest the fertility of these women regresses toward its "normal" level, that is, it declines toward the mean fertility of the larger population.

The regression artifact also occurs if the experimental group is chosen for its extreme scores on a variable that is correlated more highly (or less highly) with pretest fertility than with posttest fertility. Since program acceptance is usually positively correlated with pretest fertility but negatively correlated with posttest fertility, program acceptors usually have "abnormally" high pretest fertility. Hence their fertility regresses down toward its "normal" level on the posttest, and assigning them to the experimental group generates statistical regression that exaggerates any net program impact. In contrast, under these circumstances assigning only nonacceptors to the control group produces a group with "abnormally" low pretest fertility. Hence, on the posttest the fertility of this group regresses upward toward the mean of the larger group. The effect of this is also to exaggerate any net program impact. Although the experimental and control groups may be matched on additional variables influencing fertility, as in the case of the self-selection biases, this matching reduces the magnitude of the regression pseudo-effect, but cannot eliminate it.

In sum, two regression effects undermine the internal validity of this quasi-experiment: experimental group posttest fertility regresses downward, and control group posttest fertility regresses upward. Both act to exaggerate the program's role. Subsequent matching of the experimental and control groups reduces but does not eradicate the bias. Compared to the self-selection biases, however, the regression pseudo-effect is probably small because measurement error and random fluctuations in fertility are probably small compared to lawful differential fertility change.

## STUDIES USING THE NONEQUIVALENT CONTROL GROUP DESIGN

Ten studies of family planning programs have used nonequivalent control group quasi-experiments to assess the net fertility decline hypothesis. Four (Takeshita, Peng, and Liu, 1964; Chang, Liu, and Chow, 1969;[10] Chow, 1968; and Johnson, Tan, and Corsa, 1973) use women as the experimental units, as in the preceding example. Six others (Hermalin, 1968; Ravenholt and Chao, 1974a; Freedman and Berelson, 1976; Teachman, Hogan, and Bogue, 1978; Tsui and Bogue, 1978; and Mauldin and Berelson, 1978a) use geographical areas as the unit of analysis.

Comparing experimental and control groups, the first four studies show substantial net program impact. For Taiwan, Takeshita et al. found a 64 percent decline for acceptors versus 48 percent for nonacceptors; Chow found a 76 percent decline among acceptors, but only a 5 percent decline for married women generally; and Chang et al. found declines of 80 percent among acceptors and 48 percent among nonacceptors. Johnson et al., who conducted their study in West Malaysia, noted that the age-specific marital fertility rates of acceptors before acceptance were greater than those of married women generally, but considerably less following acceptance.

Self-selection and statistical regression biases are the major internal validity threats to these four studies (Table 1). The studies by Takeshita et al. and Chang et al. suffer two self-selection biases because in each study both treatment groups are self-selected. The research by Chow and the study by Johnson et al. eliminate one of these biases by using all married women as the control group. In all four studies matching mitigates the resulting pseudo-effects to the extent that the matching criteria fully and completely measure all nonpro-

# Validity Threats to Nonequivalent Control Group Quasi-Experiments Using Women as Experimental Units

| Sample & threat | Research | | | |
|---|---|---|---|---|
| | Takeshita et al. (1964) | Chang et al. (1969) | Chow (1968) | Johnson et al. (1973) |
| Sample | Taiwan<br>E = acceptors<br>C = nonacceptors | Taiwan<br>E = acceptors<br>C = nonacceptors | Taiwan<br>E = acceptors<br>C = all married women | West Malaysia<br>E = acceptors<br>C = all married women |
| **History/Maturation** | | | | |
| Nature of bias | none apparent, comparison of experimental group and control group fertility declines allows effects of history and maturation per se to be distinguished from any net program effect | | | |
| Direction of bias | 0 | 0 | 0 | 0 |
| **Self-selection** | | | | |
| Nature of bias | self-selection into treatment groups | self-selection into treatment groups | self-selection into experimental group | self-selection into experimental group |
| Mitigating factors | controls sex & marital composition, matches on age, marriage duration, no. of living children & sons, pregnancy status | controls sex & marital composition, matches on age, education, open interval, no. of live births | controls sex & marital composition, matches on age | controls sex & marital composition, matches on age |
| Direction of bias | + | + | + | + |
| **Statistical regression** | | | | |
| Nature of bias | E fertility regresses down, C fertility regresses up | E fertility regresses down, C fertility regresses up | E fertility regresses down | E fertility regresses down |
| Mitigating factors | same as in self-selection | same as in self-selection | same as in self-selection | same as in self-selection |
| Direction of bias | + | + | + | + |

E = experimental group
C = control group

+ = bias exaggerates net program effect
0 = magnitude of any existing bias is negligible

gram causes of differential fertility change. Compared to the research by Chow and Johnson et al., the studies by Takeshita et al. and Chang et al. control by matching a larger number of variables, but each also suffers from two, instead of one, self-selection bias. Because the composite effect of the biases and matching is difficult to assess, the overall relative severity of the pseudo-effects for each study cannot be determined. Nevertheless, they unavoidably exaggerate any net program impact. Similar reasoning applies to regression artifacts, given that fertility suffers some measurement error and/or random fluctuation. Hence, these studies necessarily underestimate indigenous fertility decline and overestimate net program efficacy.

The six nonequivalent control group studies that use geographical areas as experimental units also report substantial support for the net fertility decline hypothesis. Hermalin (1968) classifies 282 geographic areas in Taiwan as urban or rural and analyzes each set with path analysis. The dependent variable is the total fertility rate in 1965. The three measures of program strength are: the number of health workers per capita, the number of doctors per capita, and the family planning program acceptance rate. Nonprogram fertility determinants analyzed are population density, percent of females at least twelve years old with at least primary education, the crude death rate for 1963, and the total fertility rates for 1961 and 1963. Geographic areas with strong programs constitute the experimental group; those with weak programs form the control group. In summarizing the results of this study Hermalin states "This [program] effect is due not simply to the family planning program's relationship to modernizing trends in Taiwan but rather appears to represent a net contribution to fertility control beyond these other factors" (Hermalin, 1968: 11).

The second study analyzing geographic areas contrasts "fertility changes during the decade of the 1960s in 12 developing countries with relatively vigorous family planning programs for part or all of this period as against changes in 12 countries without vigorous family planning programs during this period" (Ravenholt and Chao, 1974a: 217). The fertility measures used are age-specific and total fertility rates. After discussing these data Ravenholt and Chao (1974a: 223; 1974b: J–22) conclude: "Although a number of factors may influence fertility over the long run . . . the most important single factor in attainment of sharp fertility declines is the *availability* of more effective methods of fertility control distributed through vigorous nation-wide family planning programs."

A third study analyzes nearly 30 third world countries with correlation techniques (Freedman and Berelson, 1976). The dependent variable is crude birth rate decline between 1960 and 1973. Program effort is measured by a single index. The three modernization measures used are infant mortality, school enrollment, and per capita gross domestic product.

In a fourth study Teachman, Hogan, and Bogue (1978) use correlation and regression to study the 23 departmentos of Colombia. The dependent variable is the total fertility rate in 1973. Program strength is measured as the percent of fecund, exposed, nonpregnant women who were currently protected by family planning program supplied contraception. Social and economic development are measured by the total fertility rate in 1969, the percent urban in 1973, and the percent literate in 1973. The authors conclude that the program accounts for about 21 percent of the average total fertility rate decline, net of other variables.

Tsui and Bogue (1978), in a fifth study, analyze the variation in the total fertility rate for 89 third world countries as of 1975. The independent variables analyzed are the total fertility rate, the per capita GNP, the percent urban, the infant mortality rate, the percent of employed females in agriculture, and the female school enrollment ratio, all for 1968. A fifteen item index measures family planning program strength.

Finally, Mauldin and Berelson (1978a) analyze variation in the percent decline in the crude birth rate for 89 third world countries. The seven indicators of social and economic development they analyze are adults literate, primary and secondary school enrollment, life expectancy, the infant mortality rate, the percent of males aged 15–64 in the nonagricultural labor force, the GNP per capita, and the percent of population in cities of 100,000 plus. Program strength is measured with a fifteen item index. In accounting for the variation in fertility decline, Mauldin and Berelson (1978a: 123) conclude by attributing 15–20 percent of the variation to the efforts of the family planning program, independent of other factors.

Although geographic areas rather than women form the treatment groups in these studies, because they are nonequivalent control group quasi-experiments, they are subject to most of the internal validity threats that marred the preceding four studies. The earlier discussion must simply be recast to the more aggregated unit of analysis.[11] Another distinguishing feature of three of these studies is the use of path analysis or regression/correlation. The basic arguments are little changed by this fact; they must refer to variables that vary continuously, instead of discretely.

Self-selection biases seriously threaten these studies because program strength was not randomly assigned to geographic areas. As discussed above, all the nonprogram factors that influence people's reproductive motivation and the desire to adopt birth control methods thereby influence the number of contraceptives that a family plan-

## Table 2
## Validity Threats to Nonequivalent Control Group Quasi-Experiments Using Geographic Areas as Experimental Units

| Sample & threat | Hermalin (1968) | Ravenholt & Chao (1974a) | Freedman & Berelson (1976) | Teachman et al. (1978) | Tsui & Bogue (1978) | Mauldin & Berelson (1978a) |
|---|---|---|---|---|---|---|
| Sample | Taiwan's geographic areas; E = strong program areas; C = weak program areas | 24 third world countries; E = strong programs; C = weak programs | Nearly 30 third world countries; E = strong program; C = weak program | 23 departmentos of Colombia; E = strong program areas; C = weak program areas | 89 third world countries; E = strong programs; C = weak programs | 89 third world countries; E = strong programs; C = weak programs |
| **History/Maturation** | | | | | | |
| Nature of bias | none apparent, comparison of experimental group and control group fertility declines allows effects of history and maturation per se to be distinguished from any net program effect | | | | | |
| Direction of bias | 0 | 0 | 0 | 0 | 0 | 0 |
| **Self-selection** | | | | | | |
| Nature of bias | self-selection into treatment groups | self-selection into treatment groups | self-selection into treatment groups | self-selection into treatment groups | self-selection into treatment groups | self-selection into treatment groups |
| Mitigating factors | controls age-sex composition, density, statistically controls preprogram TFR, CDR, density, female education | controls age-sex composition (informal discussion of social and economic development) | statistically controls infant mortality, school enrollment, per capita gross domestic product | controls age-sex composition, statistically controls preprogram TFR, % urban, % literate | controls age-sex composition, statistically controls preprogram TFR, per capita GNP, % urban, infant mortality, % employed females in agriculture, female school enrollment ratio | controls age-sex composition, marital patterns, statistically controls adults literate, primary and secondary school enrollment, life expectancy, infant mortality, % males aged 15-64 in nonagricultural labor force, GNP per capita, % population in cities of 100,000+ |

Research

| Direction of bias | + | + | + | + | + | + | + |
| Statistical regression | | | | | | | |
| Direction of bias | 0 | 0 | 0 | 0 | 0 | 0 | 0 |

E = experimental group
C = control group
+ = bias exaggerates net program effect
0 = magnitude of any existing bias is negligible

ning program is able to distribute, and hence the extent to which a program, once implemented, will grow and flourish.

In addition, for analyses at the subnational but particularly the national level the political receptivity of a population to birth control, which is determined by a broad array of nonprogram factors, can have a major impact on whether or not, and with what vigor, the political leaders of a society pursue a policy to implement family planning programs (Demerath, 1976; Stycos, 1971). In this fashion, entire societies are self-selected for program strength. Finally, through their influence on the extent to which a country has a well-developed transportation and communications infrastructure, a broad array of nonprogram factors have a major impact on the ability of a nation to create and maintain family planning distribution centers and communications strategies. In this fashion too, entire societies are self-selected for program strength.

For these reasons, program strength in different geographic areas is influenced by all lawful determinants of fertility and contraceptive usage, and by a variety of additional factors. Consequently, geographic areas that would have experienced major fertility reductions and high contraceptive usage without the program generated strong programs, but areas that would have experienced little or no fertility decreases generated weaker programs (Table 2). Because geographic areas are self-selected for program strength, support for the net fertility decline hypothesis is exaggerated in these studies.[12]

Statistical regression, however, is virtually nonexistent in these studies. First, its magnitude depends on the extent of random fluctuation and measurement error, but these are comparatively small when geographic areas replace individual women as the experimental subjects. Second, its magnitude is inversely related to the pretest-posttest fertility correlation, but in these studies of geographic areas this correlation is quite high. Hence, the regression artifact must be quite small. Third, the regression bias is directly related to the difference between the correlations of acceptance with the pretest and the posttest. Since these correlations are similar, their difference is quite small, and the regression artifact is also quite small. Finally, additional control variables further reduce the size of any existing regression bias.[13] Nevertheless, the self-selection biases act to exaggerate any independent program effect.

## STUDIES USING THE ONE-GROUP PRETEST-POSTTEST DESIGN

The indigenous and net fertility decline hypotheses also have been assessed with "one-group pretest-posttest designs," which differ from the preceding type in that only one treatment group—an experimental group—is utilized. The design requires the selection of the experimental group, a pretest, exposure to the program, and a posttest. If posttest fertility is less than pretest fertility, support for the net fertility decline hypothesis is inferred. Of the one-group studies reviewed here, those which combine the one-group design with life table analysis of IUD use-effectiveness are the most ingenious (Potter, 1969; Wolfers, 1969).

Using these methods to study Taiwan, Potter develops three sets of estimates of the "births averted per first segment of IUD" (Potter, 1969: 418).[14] The first set of estimates is derived assuming that no birth control would have been practiced had the program not existed.[15] The second (medium) and third (conservative) sets of estimates, which bear on the net fertility decline hypothesis, use somewhat different experimental groups.[16]

The medium set is derived, essentially, by comparing the pretest and posttest fertility of all program acceptors in the sample.[17] As Potter notes (1969: 428), the inference that the entire fertility decline of acceptors was generated by the program requires the assumption that without the program their fertility would not have changed. But Taiwan was in the midst of rapid socioeconomic change prior to and during the period analyzed, and Taiwanese fertility had been decreasing for several years before program implementation. Hence, it seems likely that the historical/maturational decline would have continued without the program, and that the medium estimate exaggerates the program's net impact (Table 3).

Self-selection biases in this study act in the same direction because only program acceptors are assigned to the experimental group. To the extent that measured fertility is in error or fluctuates randomly, the selection procedure also produces a statistical regression pseudo-effect to magnify the program's efficacy. All these biases are diminished only to the extent that the control variables perfectly measure all nonprogram causes of differential fertility (Table 3).

Potter's conservative estimate suffers the same flaws, but to a lesser degree. Instead of using all program acceptors for the pretest fertility measure, it uses a subset of them: program acceptors who sometime before the advent of the family planning program had used a birth control method.[18] Compared to the *pretest* fertility of all acceptors, then, this subset of all acceptors has relatively low *pretest* fertility due to *preprogram* differential fertility determinants. But as Potter (1969: 428) indicates, this will completely eliminate the history, maturation, self-selection, and statistical regression biases only if the following assumption is valid: had the program not existed, the posttest fertility of all acceptors would have equalled the pretest fertility of the subset

**Table 3**
**Validity Threats to One-Group Pretest-Posttest Quasi-Experiments**

| Sample & threat | Potter (1969) medium | Potter (1969) conservative | Research Wolfers (1969) | Lee & Isbister (1966) | Balakrishnan (1973) |
|---|---|---|---|---|---|
| Sample | Taiwan, E = acceptors | Taiwan, E/Pre = previous contraceptive users, E/Post = program acceptors | Singapore, E/Post=acceptors, C/Pre-Post = married women | Republic of Korea E = acceptors | Barbados, E/Pre = all women, E/Post = acceptors |
| **History/Maturation** | | | | | |
| Nature of bias | Without a control group to compare to the experimental group, probable fertility decline due to historical events and maturation in the absence of the program is confounded with any net program effect | | | | |
| Mitigating factors | controls age-sex & marital status composition, nonprogram sterilization, spouse death, divorce, amenorrhea, IUD loss from pregnancy, expulsion or removal, and only in conservative design E/pre further self-selected for previous contraceptive use | | controls age-sex & marital status composition, post-partum & secondary sterili-ty, pregnancy, IUD loss from removal or expulsion, allows reinsertions (see text regarding control group) | controls age-sex & marital status composition, mortality, widow-hood | controls age-sex composition |
| Direction of bias | + | + | + | + | + |
| **Self-selection** | | | | | |
| Nature of bias | self-selection into experimental group | self-selection into experimental groups | self-selection into E/post | self-selection into experimental group | self-selection into E/post |
| Mitigating factors | same as history/maturation | same as history/maturation | same as history/maturation | same as history/maturation | same as history/maturation & E/pre-selected as all women |

| | | | | |
|---|---|---|---|---|
| Direction of bias | + | + | + | + | + |

| | | | | | |
|---|---|---|---|---|---|
| Statistical regression | | | | | |
| Nature of bias | E fertility regresses down | E fertility regresses down | E/post fertility regresses down | E fertility regresses down | E fertility regresses down |
| Mitigating factors | same as self-selection | same as self-selection | same as self-selection | same as self-selection | same as self-selection |
| Direction of bias | + | + | + | + | + |

E = experimental group
C = control group
Pre = pretest
Post = posttest
+ = bias exaggerates net program effect
? = direction of any existing bias is unknown

who sometime earlier in their lives used birth control. But there is reason to doubt the validity of this assumption.

All the posttest group chose to employ contraceptives throughout the entire posttest period. In contrast, although all the pretest women employed contraception sometime prior to the program, a potentially large proportion of them were not using contraception during a substantial portion of the three to five year pretest period. Insofar as this difference in usage is due to indigenous socioeconomic conditions, the procedures employed do not fully compensate for the biases produced by using acceptors as the single treatment group. This line of reasoning implies that history, maturation, self-selection, and regression biases exaggerate support for the net fertility decline hypothesis in the conservative estimate, though to a lesser degree than the medium estimate.

The empirical results of the Potter research uphold this argument. For a period of IUD retention extending beyond six years, the net number of births averted per first segment of IUD is .64 for the medium estimate and .43 for the conservative estimate. These results exceed in magnitude the estimate of .371 developed by Chang, Liu, and Chow (1969) for approximately a four year period. This comparison suggests that the conservative estimate is about as biased as the estimate developed by Chang, Liu, and Chow (Table 1), and that the medium estimate is considerably more biased.

Analyzing Singapore's fertility change, Wolfers (1969) also combines the life table techniques developed by Potter with additional calculations. Because the design is a hybrid of the nonequivalent control group and one-group pretest-postest, its internal validity is a hybrid of the validities of the pure designs. This research uses a pretest and posttest for the control group (all married women), but only a posttest for the experimental group (program acceptors).

The specific calculations assume that without the program the acceptor fertility decline would have equalled that of all married women.[19] Although the time period of the married women's fertility decline is not explicitly stated in the test discussion, it may be assumed to correspond to the pretest-posttest period. If so, the research is not marred by threats of history and maturation because the rate at which married women remove themselves from exposure to the risk of giving birth due to historical and maturational forces is applied to acceptors. However, if control group data are for only the preprogram period, both validity threats may undermine the research (Table 3). In either case, assigning only program acceptors to the experimental group generates self-selection biases, which, despite control variables that reduce their severity, exaggerate the net fertility decline. Statistical regression produces a similar pseudo-effect, if, as seems likely, the pretest fertility of the experimental group was greater than that of married women generally (Table 3).

The two remaining one-group pretest-posttest studies were conducted by Lee and Isbister (1966: 737–758) on the Republic of Korea and by Balakrishnan (1973: 353–364) on Barbados. Program acceptors are the experimental group used by Lee and Isbister, and Balakrishnan uses calculations that in effect compare the preprogram (1954–1960) fertility of all women by age with the posttest fertility (1961–1970) of acceptors by age. Lacking a control group and using acceptors as the experimental group, these studies muddle the effects of history, maturation, self-selection, and regression with any net program effect.

In the Lee and Isbister study control variables reduce but do not eliminate these problems. The Balakrishnan study mitigates the impact of these biases by basing the pretest on all women, not just acceptors. Some bias remains, however, because acceptors are more strongly selected for nonprogram causes of fertility decline than are all women. Because Balakrishnan (1973: 359) also considers the net program effect to be exaggerated, a more realistic estimate of the number of births averted is obtained by multiplying estimates for various years by proportions ranging from 0.3 to 0.6. It is unfortunate that the derivation of these proportions is not described, and hence cannot be evaluated.

In sum, all five one-group pretest-posttest studies are marred by internal validity threats that, insofar as their direction can be determined, provide unfounded support for the net fertility decline hypothesis.

## STUDIES USING THE POSTTEST-ONLY CONTROL GROUP DESIGN

The "posttest-only control group design" is similar to the nonequivalent control group design, except no pretest is conducted. This difference has implications for the nature of potential validity threats. Potter, Freedman, and Chow (1968: 852–853) use this design to evaluate the Taiwanese program through 1966 by assigning program acceptors to the experimental group and all married women to the control group. Although the age-specific fertility of the experimental group was much lower, a net program effect should not be inferred, because self-selection undermines the study.[20] History and maturation as such do not mar the study because the control group provides a posttest baseline for comparison, and regression is a negligible problem because the treatment groups are compared only on the posttest after the experimental group (acceptor) fertility has regressed toward the mean of the control group (all married women). However, the experimental group consisting only of program acceptors is self-selected for inordinately low posttest fertility due to history and maturation for reasons similar to those that apply to the nonequivalent control group design.

Also using a posttest-only control group design, Freedman and Takeshita (1969: 147, 306–309) conclude in part, *"Taichung's fertility decline was accelerated in the year following the [program introduction], and for 1963–1964 exceeded that of other cities of the province by a considerable margin (1969: 147)."* The total fertility rate comparisons employed are the most adequate for present purposes. Taichung is the experimental group, and four other major Taiwanese cities lacking a program are the control group.

Although self-selection is not a threat here since none of the available evidence suggests that Taichung was chosen for study because of unusual fertility change (Table 4), the study is marred by a regression artifact called instability. Some instability is present in any time series, and if the fertility change during a particular year lies within the limits of normal instability, then instability is a plausible rival to the net program effect hypothesis. This occurs in the present study. Although the Taichung total fertility rate decreased twice as rapidly as in other cities between 1963 and 1964, fertility declined more than three times as rapidly in the other cities than in Taichung during the preceding year. This suggests the inferred program effect is within the normal range of instability, and statistical regression explains the apparent program effect.[21]

Bean and Seltzer (1968) discuss research on Pakistan that calculates the "couple years of protection" afforded to couples during a given year in order to estimate the total number of years that the women were effectively protected from the risk of giving birth due to program supplied methods.[22] The couple years of protection estimate is divided by three to estimate the total number of births averted on the assumption that three couple years of protection prevents a birth. This corresponds to a posttest-only control group study where it is assumed that experimental group fertility is zero, and that the control group has one birth for every three women in the experimental group. Mauldin (1967: 78) and Bean and Seltzer (1968: 948–954) observe that the couple years of protection index is based on quite limited data, and Bean and Seltzer further indicate that the ratio of three couple years of protection per one birth averted lacks empirical foundation. Hence, the research does not provide a meaningful estimate of the net program effect and may be plagued by all the internal validity threats discussed herein, although their direction and magnitude cannot be determined (Table 4).

Also using posttest-only control group designs King et al. (1974: 149–163) analyze 16 states of India, and Srikantan (1977: 70–160) conducts two analyses, one including 20 third world countries worldwide, and another including 10 third world countries in East and Southeast Asia. These analyses, which employ path analysis/regression/correlation techniques, can be viewed as assuming models in which each causally prior variable influences all later variables, both independently and through all succeeding variables.[23] The exogenous demographic or socioeconomic variables influence program input/output variables, and they all influence fertility. Although control variables reduce the self-selection bias in these studies, the experimental groups—in effect the areas with strong programs—are self-selected for low fertility, and the control groups—in effect areas with weak programs—are self-selected for high fertility, and any program effect is overestimated.

In sum, one of the posttest-only studies depends on very limited data, and insofar as the direction of biases to the remaining studies can be identified, they overstate any net program impact.

## STUDIES USING THE INTERRUPTED TIME SERIES DESIGN

An "interrupted time series design" is, for present purposes, a series of (two or more) fertility measurements, followed by program implementation, followed by another series of fertility measurements. If a discontinuity in fertility occurs when the program is introduced, the program is inferred to have generated a net fertility change. This design is formally superior to those above because fewer internal validity threats undermine it. Self-selection and statistical regression biases do not plague the design if, as in the studies here, the experimental group is the entire population exposed to a family planning program. The maturation threat is small because the preprogram time series allows pretreatment maturation to be assessed. If preprogram and postprogram fertility changes are similar, we infer maturation produced both, but if postprogram fertility change is greater, the program is inferred to have produced the difference.[24] With a longer preprogram time series, which allows maturational change to be gauged more accurately, the threat is more effectively reduced. History does undermine this study, however, because without a control group its effect on fertility after program implementation cannot be distinguished from program generated change.

Studying Hong Kong, Freedman and Adlakha (1968) find that for most ages marital fertility declined more rapidly following the program (1965–1966) than prior to it (1961–1965).[25] Moreover, marital

# Table 4
## Validity Threats to Posttest-Only Control Group Quasi-Experiments

<table>
<tr><th rowspan="2">Sample & threat</th><th colspan="6">Research</th></tr>
<tr><th>Potter, Freedman & Chow (1968)</th><th>Freedman & Takeshita (1969: 301-302)</th><th>Freedman & Takeshita (1969: 147, 306-309)</th><th>Bean & Seltzer (1968)</th><th>King et al. (1974: 149-163)</th><th>Srikantan (1977)</th></tr>
<tr><td>Sample</td><td>Taiwan<br>E = acceptors<br>C = married women</td><td>Taichung, Taiwan<br>E = acceptors<br>C = married women</td><td>Taiwan, E = Taichung, C = Taipei, Tainan & Kellung</td><td>Pakistan, by assumption E = 0 fertility, C = 1 births/3 women</td><td>16 Indian states<br>E = strong programs<br>C = weak programs</td><td>10 & 20 third world countries<br>E = strong programs<br>C = weak programs</td></tr>
<tr><td>History/Maturation</td><td colspan="6"></td></tr>
<tr><td>Nature of bias</td><td colspan="6">none apparent, comparison of experimental group and control group posttest fertility allows effects of history and maturation per se to be distinguished from any net program effect</td></tr>
<tr><td>Direction of bias</td><td>0</td><td>0</td><td>0</td><td>?</td><td>0</td><td>0</td></tr>
<tr><td>Self-selection</td><td colspan="6"></td></tr>
<tr><td>Nature of bias</td><td>self-selection into E</td><td>self-selection into E</td><td>none apparent</td><td>inadequate data</td><td>self-selection into E & C</td><td>self-selection into E & C</td></tr>
<tr><td>Mitigating factors</td><td>controls age-sex & marital composition</td><td>controls age-sex & marital composition</td><td>controls age-sex composition</td><td>none apparent</td><td>controls up to 4 socioeconomic indicators</td><td>controls age-sex composition & one (or ave. of several) demographic or socio-economic indicators</td></tr>
<tr><td>Direction of bias</td><td>+</td><td>+</td><td>0</td><td>?</td><td>+</td><td>+</td></tr>
</table>

Statistical
regression

| Nature of bias | none apparent | none apparent | E/C difference in normal instability range | inadequate data | none apparent | none apparent |
|---|---|---|---|---|---|---|
| Direction of bias | 0 | 0 | + | ? | 0 | 0 |

E = experimental group
C = control group
+ = bias exaggerates net program effect
0 = magnitude of any existing bias is negligible
? = direction of any existing bias is unknown

fertility change had little influence on the crude birth rate before the program, but was the major demographic component of birth rate decline later. History undermines this research[26] and similar research on Hong Kong by Wat and Hodge (1972). To reduce this problem Wat and Hodge explicitly incorporate three measures of history into their time series multiple regression analysis by regressing the crude birth rate (1951–1967) on three indicators of social and economic modernization: (1) the infant mortality rate; (2) the percentage of women among all employees in industrial establishments; and (3) the ratio of the number of children in secondary schools to the number in primary schools. Then the same multiple regression is calculated again, but with the number of new clients attending family planning clinics as an additional independent variable.[27] Inferences are drawn by comparing the two analyses.

Despite the use of three indicators of historical change, not all historical effects can be measured, and this study remains somewhat biased by history,[28] though to a lesser extent than the Freedman and Adlakha study which takes no historical forces explicitly into account. Both studies reduce the threat posed by maturation, but Wat and Hodge do so more effectively by analyzing a longer preprogram period (13 years) than the Freedman-Adlakha study (4 years).[29]

From their study Wat and Hodge (1972) conclude, "Endogenous changes in Hong Kong's socio-economic system appear to generate the observed fertility decline and leave little room for the operation of such exogenous features as family planning activities . . . . The results presented here . . . reveal that there is no decisive empirical evidence which requires one to accept the conclusion that such [program] activities were a causal factor in Hong Kong's fertility decline" (460, 464). Since the more adequate of these two studies fails to find a net program effect, the Freedman and Adlakha study, which suggests that a net program effect did occur, is apparently undermined by history to overstate program efficacy (Table 5).

For Singapore, Wolfers (1970) compares, in effect, the 1961–1965 and 1965–1969 age-specific fertility rate declines,[30] and Chang and Hauser (1975) compare annual total fertility rate declines for 1957–1966 and 1966–1970. Although both note that the postprogram decrease is more rapid and attribute the difference to the program, a more extended time series analysis shows that the program's impact was mostly transitory.[31] During 1969–70 the total fertility rate decline fell to roughly the preprogram level at 4.7 percent, the 1970–1971 decline was only 1.3 percent, and the total fertility rate increased by 0.2 percent from 1971 to 1972 (Chang and Hauser, 1975; Anderson, Cheng, and Wan, 1977). This suggests that much of the

1966–1969 net program effect reflected a temporary postponement of births, and the longer term net program effect is fairly small. Although the total fertility rate decline jumped sharply to 7.9 percent, 15.4 percent, and 11.8 percent between 1972 and 1975 (Anderson, Cheng, and Wan, 1977), this can be attributed more plausibly to government incentive and disincentive policies discussed in Chapter 1, which were instituted between 1968 and 1975, and to liberalized abortion and sterilization laws.

Studying Taiwan with an interrupted time series, Sun (1975: 475–483) compares the average annual rate of decrease in age-specific marital fertility rates for two periods, 1959–1963 and 1963–1971.[32] Although this comparison suggests a net program effect, Li (1973: 101) analyzes a much longer time series for Taiwan and finds no support for the technological hypothesis. Both studies control age-sex composition change, and the Sun study further controls marital status composition change, but without a control group history remains a problem. In the absence of direct evidence, the most reasonable assumption is that history produced the same sort of fertility decline before and after the program was implemented.

Insofar as the assumption is valid for Taiwan, the Li study more effectively takes history into consideration by analyzing a much longer preprogram period, thirteen years versus the four years of the Sun study, and by more closely approximating the accelerating nature of preprogram fertility change. For similar reasons the Li research is less threatened by maturation. These arguments suggest that Li's work, which provides no support for the technological hypothesis, is less biased than the Sun study. They also appear to account for the contradictory conclusions of the studies by Sun and by Li.

In general, conclusions from interrupted time series designs are more strongly supported than conclusions based on the preceding designs, mainly because they are not marred by self-selection and statistical regression biases. History remains a problem, however. Nonetheless, this critical review and comparison of the six interrupted time series studies, with some additional evidence for Singapore, suggests that the best of them provide little if any support for the net fertility decline hypothesis.

## A STUDY USING THE CONTROL SERIES DESIGN

The "control series quasi-experimental design," which is formally superior to those discussed above, is an interrupted time series design expanded to include a control group that is not exposed to the program, but for which preprogram and postprogram fertility series are

**Table 5**
**Validity Threats to Interrupted Time Series Quasi-Experiments**

| Sample & threat | Freedman & Adlakha (1968) | Wat & Hodge (1972) | Wolfers (1970) | Chang & Hauser (1975) | Sun (1975) | Li (1973) |
|---|---|---|---|---|---|---|
| | | | Research | | | |
| Sample | Hong Kong 1961-66, age-specific marital fertility rates | Hong Kong 1951-67, crude birth rates | Singapore 1961-69, age-specific fertility rates | Singapore 1957-70, total fertility rates | Taiwan 1959-71, age-specific marital fertility rates | Taiwan 1951-70, total fertility rates |
| **History** | | | | | | |
| Nature of bias | Without a control group, experimental group fertility decline due to historical events is confounded with any net program effect if assumed preprogram change underestimates actual postprogram historical change | | | | | |
| Mitigating factors | controls age-sex composition, attempts marital composition control | controls 3 historical factors | controls age-sex & ethnic composition | controls age-sex composition | controls age-sex & marital composition (see text) | controls age-sex composition (see text) |
| Direction of bias | + | ? | + | + | + | ? |
| **Maturation** | | | | | | |
| Nature of bias | None apparent, analysis of preprogram fertility change allows maturation to be taken into account, assuming preprogram and postprogram maturation are similar | | | | | |
| Mitigating factors | same as history & controls 4 yr. preprogram maturation | same as history & controls 13 yr. preprogram maturation | same as history & controls 4 yr. preprogram maturation | same as history & controls 8 yr. preprogram maturation | same as history & controls 4 yr. preprogram maturation | same as history & controls 13 yr. preprogram maturation |
| Direction of bias | 0 | 0 | 0 | 0 | 0 | 0 |

| Self-selection & regression | | | | | |
|---|---|---|---|---|---|
| Nature of bias | None apparent, all research studies, entire population | | | | |
| Direction of bias | 0 | 0 | 0 | 0 | 0 |

0     0     0

+ = bias exaggerates net program effect
0 = magnitude of any existing bias is negligible
? = direction of any existing bias is unknown

measured. As reflected in the following discussion this additional control group eliminates the single validity threat that plagued the interrupted time series design—history.

If both the experimental and the control group experience similar preprogram fertility change, it may be assumed that similar historical events are producing similar fertility change in both groups. Then, even if history produces a different sort of fertility change following program implementation, it can be assumed to occur in both groups. Hence, if postprogram fertility change is the same in the two treatment groups, one infers historical events generated them, and there was no net program effect. On the other hand, a more rapid fertility decline in the experimental group implies a net program effect, and its magnitude is estimated as the difference between the groups.[33]

Because the Davis (1967) research, comparing change in the general fertility rate of Taiwan before and after program implementation with similar change for Japan during the corresponding period, is a control series design, it is not undermined by any of the internal validity threats. Davis (1967: 735) suggests a "plot of the Japanese and Taiwanese birth rates shows marked similarity of the two curves, despite a difference in level." Fertility declined until roughly the end of World War II, then increased dramatically but briefly, and declined thereafter. This similarity might well be expected, since both Asian islands experienced rapid social and economic development during the period. Davis (1967: 736) concludes, "In sum, the widely acclaimed family-planning program in Taiwan may, at most, have somewhat speeded the later phase of fertility decline which would have occurred anyway because of modernization."[34] Because this conclusion is based on the strongest research design that has been used in assessing the technological hypothesis in a third world country, it carries considerable weight.

## SUMMARY

The flourishing controversy between the motivational and technological schools of thought regarding the independent impact of family planning programs on fertility in third world countries has been sustained by a stream of studies often drawing contradictory conclusions. Aimed toward the debate's resolution, this chapter critically evaluates the validity of 30 quasi-experiments bearing on the question: does the implementation of organized family planning programs that distribute contraceptive technology in third world countries generate fertility decline that is independent of other causes?

Although the exact relative validity of all 30 studies cannot be definitively determined with available data, the rank ordering that is

# Table 6
## Summary of Validity Threats to Past Research Assessing Net Program Effects for Third World Countries

| Research Design & Investigators | Experimental Unit & Country | Internal Validity Threat | | | |
|---|---|---|---|---|---|
| | | History | Maturation | Self-selection Biases | Statistical Regression |
| One-group pretest-posttest | Individual women | | | | |
| Potter (1969) medium | Taiwan | + | + | + | + |
| Potter (1969) conservative | Taiwan | + | + | + | + |
| Wolfers (1969) | Taiwan | ? | ? | + | + |
| Lee & Isbister (1966) | Republic of Korea | + | + | + | + |
| Balakrishnan (1973) | Barbados | + | + | + | + |
| Nonequivalent control group | Individual women | | | | |
| Takeshita et al. (1964) | Taiwan | 0 | 0 | + | + |
| Chang et al. (1969) | Taiwan | 0 | 0 | + | + |
| Chow (1968) | Taiwan | 0 | 0 | + | + |
| Johnson et al. (1973) | West Malaysia | 0 | 0 | + | + |
| Nonequivalent control group | Geographic areas | | | | |
| Hermalin (1968) | Taiwan | 0 | 0 | + | 0 |
| Ravenholt and Chao (1974a) | 24 third world countries | 0 | 0 | + | 0 |
| Freedman & Berelson (1976) | Nearly 30 third world countries | 0 | 0 | + | 0 |

+ = bias exaggerates net program effect
? = direction of any existing bias is unknown
0 = magnitude of any existing bias is negligible

# Table 6 continued

| Research Design & Investigators | Experimental Unit & Country | Internal Validity Threat | | | Statistical Regression |
|---|---|---|---|---|---|
| | | History | Maturation | Self-selection Biases | |
| Teachman et al. (1978) | 23 departmentos of Colombia | 0 | 0 | + | 0 |
| Tsui & Bogue (1978) | 89 third world countries | 0 | 0 | + | 0 |
| Mauldin & Berelson (1978a) | 89 third world countries | 0 | 0 | + | 0 |
| Posttest-only control group | Individual women | | | | |
| Potter, Freedman, and Chow (1968) | Taiwan | 0 | 0 | + | 0 |
| Freedman & Takeshita (1969: 301-302) | Taichung, Taiwan | 0 | 0 | + | 0 |
| Bean & Seltzer (1968) | Pakistan | ? | ? | ? | ? |
| Posttest-only control group | Geographic areas | | | | |
| Freedman & Takeshita (1969: 147, 306-309) | Taichung, Taiwan | 0 | 0 | 0 | + |
| King et al. (1974: 149-163) | 16 Indian states | 0 | 0 | + | 0 |
| Srikantan (1977) | 10 & 20 third world countries | 0 | 0 | + | 0 |
| Interrupted time series | Geographic areas | | | | |
| Freedman & Adlakha (1968) | Hong Kong | + | 0 | 0 | 0 |
| Wat & Hodge (1972) | Hong Kong | ? | 0 | 0 | 0 |
| Wolfers (1970) | Singapore | + | 0 | 0 | 0 |

| | | | | | |
|---|---|---|---|---|---|
| Chang & Hauser (1975) | Singapore | + | 0 | 0 | 0 |
| Sun (1975) | Taiwan | + | 0 | 0 | 0 |
| Li (1973) | Taiwan | ? | 0 | 0 | 0 |
| **Control series** | **Geographic areas** | | | | |
| Davis (1967) | Taiwan | 0 | 0 | 0 | 0 |

possible allows firm inferences concerning the motivational-techno-logical debate to be drawn. The least adequate studies are the one-group pretest-posttest quasi-experiments because virtually all of them are undermined by history, maturation, the three self-selection biases, and statistical regression. Since the addition of a control group elim-inates the threats of history and maturation as such, the nonequiva-lent control group quasi-experiments using women as the experimen-tal unit are considerably more adequate. Still less biased are nonequivalent control group studies that reduce the regression bias to a negligible magnitude by using geographic areas as the experimental units. These studies and all but one of the posttest-only control group studies do suffer self-selection biases which exaggerate the net pro-gram effect (Table 6).

Inferences drawn using the interrupted time series designs are con-siderably more conclusive because only history produces bias, and this only to the extent that it produces different magnitudes of fertility change prior to and following program implementation. In the more adequate of the two time series studies of Hong Kong, Wat and Hodge (1972) conclude that a net program effect has not been demonstrated. For Singapore, the time series studies by Wolfers (1970) and by Chang and Hauser (1975) find a substantial net program effect for three years, but extending their analysis a few years further shows that much of the effect was transitory, leaving relatively little long-term impact. Similarly for Taiwan, the time series analysis that is apparently more adequate indicates that the accelerated fertility decrease after the program cannot be attributed to the program (Li, 1973). Also study-ing Taiwan, Davis (1967: 736) infers little or no net program impact using a control series quasi-experiment—the best design reviewed.

Although many of the studies discussed here imply substantial net program effects, most of them employ relatively weak research de-signs which are impaired by several validity threats that *necessarily overestimate any net program impact*. In contrast the best studies find little or no support for the net fertility decline hypothesis. All things considered, for the countries studied this critical review provides sub-stantial support for the motivational school of thought and little sup-port for the technological school.

## NOTES

1. This abstract discussion of various research designs draws on Hyman (1955), Campbell and Stanley (1963), Campbell (1969), Campbell and Erle-bacher (1970a; 1970b), Rossi and Williams (1972), and Riecken and Boruch (1974). Greater deail and additional references are found in these works.

2. Geographical areas may also be used as the subjects in a study that

embodies the ideal research design. In reviewing past research that uses geographical areas as the experimental units, the corresponding ideal design serves as the standard of comparison.

3. The role of statistical tests in drawing such inferences is further discussed in references cited in footnote 1 or a standard text on statistics.

4. Random assignment of individual women would be possible only by moving some people into or out of geographical areas exposed to the family planning program. Such movement is blocked by ethical, legal, political, and administrative considerations. Although these factors would not necessarily impede the implementation of an experimental design with geographical areas as the experimental unit, such a study has not come to the attention of this author. For example, of the 111 "experiments" involving family planning programs which are discussed by Cuca and Pierce (1977), only 12 are "true experiments," that is, only 12 involve randomization and controls. None of these true experiments employs fertility as a dependent variable. Hence, they do not measure the impact of family planning programs on fertility. Furthermore, all of the eight quasi-experiments discussed by Cuca and Pierce that do employ fertility as a dependent variable find little or no program effect, suffer from severe methodological problems, and/or are based on relatively small samples of people or short periods of time.

5. The specific design outlined here is chosen for its close correspondence to actual past research. This design is named the nonequivalent control group design because experimental and control groups are compared, but their pre-experimental similarity is not insured through random assignment of subjects to treatments. Instead, the groups are known to be similar along one or more dimensions, and the pretest measures the degree to which the groups have similar fertility prior to program implementation.

6. Two broad types of validity may be distinguished: internal and external. Internal validity refers to the credibility of inferences as they bear on the specific empirical situation in which the research is conducted.

7. Fertility typically does change systematically through time.

8. Apart from involuntary fertility change.

9. They are referred to as self-selection interactions because the research procedures allow women, in effect, to self-select themselves into one of the treatment groups.

10. Chow (1969; 1970) also discusses the research.

11. Another potential threat, the ecological fallacy, is discussed by Hermalin (1968: 7).

12. Hermalin (1968) and Teachman et al. (1978) mention this self-selection process, but do not fully develop its implications for internal validity. Although these six studies reduce the magnitude of the problem by controlling, statistically or otherwise, for several nonprogram fertility determinants (Table 2), none control for all nonprogram fertility determinants, and all exaggerate any net program effect.

13. Campbell and Erlebacher (1970a: 194; 1970b: 222) and Riecken and Boruch (1974: 109) discuss the general criteria that determine the magnitude of a regression artifact.

14. Sun (1975: 460–467) and Srikantan (1977: 222–227) draw mainly on Potter's work in developing net program effect estimates.

15. Potter's method somewhat underestimates births averted by program contraception under the assumption that no birth control would have been used in the absence of the program (Clague and Ridley, 1974; Hernandez, 1975).

16. Potter, Freedman, and Chow (1968) draw heavily on this research in discussing the Taiwan program. The use of life table concepts to measure the use effectiveness of contraception is discussed by Potter (1963; 1966; 1967).

17. Although the actual mathematical calculations are rather complex, the key features of the research for present purposes can be analyzed without discussing them in detail.

18. This conclusion is drawn from Potter (1969) and from Freedman and Takeshita (1969), the source of the pretest data. Information concerning past use of birth control methods was obtained from the question, "Have you ever used any of the methods I mentioned a moment ago?" (Freedman and Takeshita, 1969: Appendix 1–3, p. 2).

19. Calculations employed are intended to approximate the fertility decline of all married women. See Wolfers (1969) for actual procedures.

20. Freedman and Takeshita (1969: 301–302) use the same design, except that the control group is all married women in Taichung instead of Taiwan. This difference might subject the Freedman and Takeshita research to greater experimental mortality and differential migration. Comparing the empirical results of the two studies suggests, however, that the Freedman and Takeshita study is less biased since the estimated net program effect is smaller. The difference probably lies in the control groups used.

21. For a more detailed comparison with the same conclusion see Li (1973).

22. Wishik (1967: 15–21; 1970) developed the couple years of protection index.

23. The Srikantan (1977) study explicitly develops this model, but the King et al. (1974: 149) research "does not seek to find structural relationships or to identify cause-effect linkages; the available data do not permit consideration of all the independent variables that need to be included to formulate a structural model."

24. This assumes maturation is gradual and steady.

25. Freedman, et al. (1969; 1970) extend the analysis through 1968.

26. The use of marital fertility eliminates the potentially confounding effect of historical change in the female marital composition; but the marital composition may be poorly measured. Freedman, et al. (1970: 17–18) observe, "Mr. K.C. Chan suggests that variations in the rate of decline since 1965 may be caused partly by variations in the number of new marriages resulting from attempts to avoid 'blind years,' i.e., years without a spring day. We intend to explore this possibility by examining the age distribution of registered marriages, as well as their number, in relation to survey data on the distribution of intervals between marriage and first birth. Unfortunately, this effort is complicated by the fact that an estimated 40 percent of the marriages are not registered, and the time trend for this percentage is not determined."

27. Due to lack of data the second regression begins with the 1952 crude birth rate.

28. Perhaps the most obvious omissions are the failure to incorporate age and marital composition change. Aware of this, Wat and Hodge (1972: 457) suggest that "on the basis of previous work by Freedman and his associates, we may surmise that the main effect of standardization [of the crude birth rate for change in age and marital status] would be to attenuate the observed decline in the crude birth rate between 1961 and 1965. Consequently, the use of the crude birth rate will tend to exaggerate the impact of variables, such as the extension of family planning services, which were moving synchronously with the crude birth rate during these years."

29. Although Freedman and Adlakha formally control for the maturational effect of change in the age and marital status composition, the attempted control probably does not make the research more internally valid than that of Wat and Hodge (1972), as discussed in footnotes 26 and 28.

30. See Wolfers (1968; 1970) for the specific calculations.

31. In light of the apparently transitory effect of the program, further examination of Singapore to assess more thoroughly the history threat is not pursued here.

32. See Sun (1975: 475–483) for the method of calculation. Among the fertility indicators analyzed the most adequate for present purposes is age-specific marital fertility.

33. Moreover, the reasoning is identical with regard to maturation, self-selection, and statistical regression biases. Of course, the distinct effects of the rival hypotheses embodied in each of these potential validity threats cannot be separately identified. Instead, the various assumptions are subsumed under a single general assumption that without the program the relative fetility change of the treatment groups during the preprogram period would have continued during the post-implementation period. If entire populations exposed and not exposed to the program are studied, this argument need not be invoked for self-selection and regression biases, and as noted in the discussion of the interrupted time series design, the maturational threat is eliminated simply by comparing the preprogram and postprogram time series of the experimental group. The above argument suggests, however, that the inclusion of the control group in the comparison series design provides additional evidence that these potential threats are not efficacious.

34. It should be noted, however, that this research does not derive explicit empirical estimates of either the indigenous or the net program effect. Nonetheless, the conclusions drawn are similar to those from the most adequate interrupted time series study of Taiwan—the program had little net effect on fertility.

# 3

## A Demographic Approach to Estimating the Indigenous Effect and the Net Program Effect for Individual Third World Countries

Beginning with this chapter attention turns to estimating indigenous and net program effects for individual third world countries. Four countries are studied, Taiwan, South Korea, Costa Rica, and Mauritius, primarily because they have appeared to many observers to have relatively successful programs. Although the assessment in Chapter 2 indicates that the best research design for deriving indigenous and net program effect estimates is the control series design, this design cannot be implemented for these countries because appropriate control countries do not exist for each. Given this situation, the interrupted time series design is the best that can be implemented for all four countries.[1] In order to take full advantage of the strengths of this design, two types of demographic procedures are combined in a single approach. Briefly, this approach begins with a variation of direct standardization procedures to decompose crude birth rate (CBR) decline into three components, and then employs demographic projection procedures to obtain estimates of the magnitude of indigenous effects and net program effects on CBR decline.

### DECOMPOSING CRUDE BIRTH RATE DECLINE

More specifically, this approach begins by decomposing CBR decline into three distinct components: (1) decline due to the changing age-sex composition, (2) decline due to the changing marital status composition, and (3) decline due to the changing age-sex marital status specific fertility rates (Figure 1). During time intervals studied in the case studies presented below, a CBR reduction generated by age-sex composition change, that is, change in the proportion of people in various age and sex categories, is independent of the family planning program.

Of course during the first 15 years of a family planning program, the program might influence the size of the population less than 15 years old at the end of the period. A program-generated fertility decline would tend to reduce the proportion of the population under 15, and increase the proportion over 15. By increasing the proportion of the population in the childbearing ages, such program-induced change would *increase* rather than decrease the CBR, and hence could not

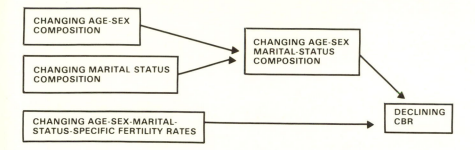

Figure 1. Decomposition of Crude Birth Rate Decline

through its influence on the age-sex structure account for CBR *decline*. Consequently, CBR decline associated with age-sex composition change must be attributed to the indigenous fertility decline hypothesis.

Similarly, because CBR decrease from change in the marital status composition is not program generated, but instead approximates the CBR reduction due to the changing population distribution with respect to the three intermediate variables—age of entry into sexual unions, permanent celibacy, and amount of reproductive period spent after or between unions—it also must be assigned to the indigenous fertility decline hypothesis.

In contrast, CBR decline due to changing age-sex marital status specific fertility rates may result from either indigenous causes or the family planning program. Before discussing the procedure used to assign composition-specific fertility rate change to one of these causes, the types of results obtained from the decomposition analysis require closer examination.

The general method for decomposing the difference between two rates into two compositional effects and a composition-specific rate effect was developed by Kitagawa (1955), extended by Retherford and Cho (1973), and refined by Das Gupta (1978). Applying the Das Gupta formulation to the Taiwanese CBR decline between 1964 and 1975 provides the following results (Table 7). First, across all ages the age-sex composition change accounts for 1 percent of the CBR decline, given the 1964–1975 average of all other factors analyzed. Second, across all ages the marital status composition change accounts for 11 percent of the CBR decline, assuming the average 1964–1975 values of other factors. Third, composition-specific fertility rate changes account for 88 percent of the decline, given the average 1964–1975 population distribution.

The more detailed age-specific results in Table 7 illustrate the possibility that change in these factors may in some empirical cases act to produce CBR increase, instead of decrease. For example, the overall rate effect is the result of two kinds of countervailing composition-specific rate effects. Rising age-specific marital fertility rates for married women aged 15–19 and 20–24 tended to increase the CBR. This

**Table 7**
**Decomposition of Crude Birth Rate Decline in Taiwan Expressed as Percentages by Age for 1964 to 1975**

| Percent of decline due to | Age of married woman | | | | | | | |
|---|---|---|---|---|---|---|---|---|
|  | All ages | 15-19 | 20-24 | 25-29 | 30-34 | 35-39 | 40-44 | 45-49 |
| Age-sex effect | 1 | 0 | -11 | 8 | 5 | 0 | -1 | 0 |
| Marital status effect | 11 | 4 | 10 | 0 | -2 | -1 | 0 | 0 |
| Rate effect | 88 | -10 | -3 | 32 | 36 | 23 | 9 | 1 |
| Total | 100 | -6 | -4 | 40 | 39 | 22 | 8 | 1 |

[a]Because the only age-sex marital status categories of the Taiwanese population that experience non-zero fertility rates are married women aged 15-49, only these women are included in Table 7.

The values of all components for the remaining age-sex marital status categories are zero. Unknown births by age of mother are distributed proportionally to known births by age of mother.

Source: Republic of China, 1973; 1975a; 1976.

tendency, however, was more than offset by the countervailing tendency of falling age-specific marital fertility rates for women aged 25–29 and older to generate CBR decrease. Hence, overall change in composition-specific rates produced 88 percent of the CBR decline. Similarly, in this case the overall effect of age-sex composition change is the sum of competing effects attributed to married women of various ages, and the overall marital status effect is the sum of opposing effects for married women of different ages.

Although CBR decline related to change in the age-sex and marital status compositions is readily attributed to the indigenous fertility decline hypothesis, the remaining CBR decline, which is related to composition-specific fertility rate change, might be due to either the program or indigenous causes.

## ANALYZING COMPOSITION-SPECIFIC FERTILITY RATE CHANGE

The second stage of the research design is a procedure for allocating composition-specific fertility rate change to the indigenous and net fertility decline hypotheses. This procedure involves projecting pre-program fertility change into the post-implementation period, and comparing projected fertility to actual fertility. If the actual post-implementation fertility rate is less than the projected rate, the difference, over and above what might have been expected from indigenous factors, is attributed to the family planning program. On the other hand, if the actual fertility rate is greater than or equal to the projected rate, no net effect is attributed to the program. In either case, any composition-specific fertility rate change that is not inferred to be a net program effect is instead attributed to indigenous causes (Figure 2).

This inferential process rests on one major assumption: if the program had not been introduced the kind of fertility change occurring before the program would have continued. Since the fertility change before the program results from a combination of changing family size goals, changing availability of birth control, and involuntary fertility change, the assumption implies that without the program these three nonprogram causes would have continued in combination to produce the same sort of fertility change they produced prior to program implementation.

More specifically, the procedures employed in this process are the following. First, preprogram fertility change is projected into the post-implementation period. Second, if actual fertility is greater than or equal to the corresponding projected fertility, then no program effect is inferred and all fertility change is allotted to indigenous causes. If

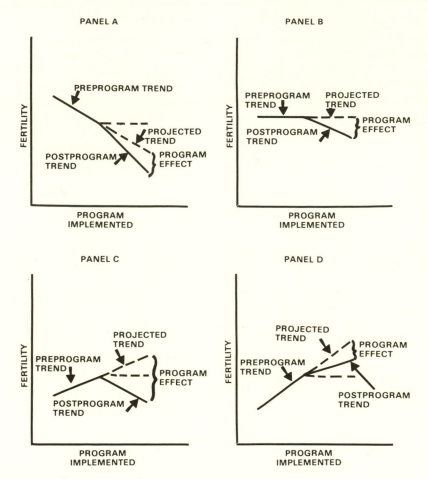

Figure 2. Situations with Net Family Planning Program Effect on Composition-Specific Fertility Rate

actual fertility is less than projected fertility, however, the difference is attributed to the program. To obtain the program effect for each year an effect occurred, the actual births ($AB_i$) and projected births ($PB_i$) are derived. The net program births averted ($NPBA_i$) is then calculated by subtracting actual from projected births. Finally, the total net program births averted for all years are derived by summing the $NPBA_i$ for each year. These calculations are summarized in Equations (1) and (2) below.

$$NPBA_i = PB_i - AB_i \qquad (1)$$
$$TNPBA = \Sigma NPBA_i \qquad (2)$$

Although the *remaining calculations are identical* in all program impact situations, their *interpretation varies* somewhat depending on the nature of the situation. Three cases may be distinguished.

In the first case actual post-implementation fertility declines and projected fertility declines or remains constant (Figure 2, Panels A and B). In this context the actual births averted by all causes ($ABA_i$) is calculated for each year by subtracting the actual births ($AB_i$) from the births that would have occurred if the fertility rate had remained constant ($CB_i$). Then the total births averted by all causes for all years (TBA) is obtained by summing the actual births averted for each year. Next the proportion of all births averted that is attributable to the program (PNPBA) is calculated by dividing the total net program births averted (TNPBA) by the total births averted by all causes (TBA). This estimates the proportion of the decline in the composition-specific fertility rate that is a net program effect.

Finally, the percentage of the CBR decline due to change in the particular composition-specific fertility rate (RA) and obtained from the decomposition procedure is multiplied by the PNPBA to estimate the net program effect on the CBR through its impact on the composition-specific rate (NPE). These calculations are summarized symbolically in Equations (3) through (6).

$$ABA_i = CB_i - AB_i \qquad (3)$$
$$TBA = \Sigma ABA_i \qquad (4)$$
$$PNPBA = TNPBA/TBA \qquad (5)$$
$$NPE = (RA)(PNPBA) \qquad (6)$$

In the second case post-implementation fertility declines but projected fertility increases (Figure 2, Panel C). The total births averted by all causes is obtained again by subtracting actual births from births occurring with constant fertility for each year and summing across years. The proportion of all births averted that is attributable to the program (PNPBA) is again calculated by dividing program averted births by total births averted (TBA), but the value is greater than 1.0 because TNPBA is greater than TBA. This value implies that the program generated all the observed composition-specific fertility rate decline and, furthermore, that without the program the fertility rate would have increased rather than decreased. Despite this difference in interpretation from the preceding case, in this case the net effect on the CBR of the program acting through the specific fertility rate also may be calculated by multiplying PNBA by RA. These calculations may be summarized as follows.

$$ABA_i = CB_i - AB_i \qquad (7)$$
$$TBA = \Sigma ABA_i \qquad (8)$$
$$PNPBA = TNPBA/TBA \qquad (9)$$
$$NPE = (RA)(PNPBA) \qquad (10)$$

Finally, in the third case both post-implementation and projected fertility increase (Figure 2, Panel D). Here the net CBR impact of the program is estimated as in the two preceding cases but the interpretation is somewhat different. Once again actual births for each year are subtracted from births occurring if fertility had remained constant, and these differences are summed across years. The result in this case, however, is interpreted to be the total additional births (TBA*) produced by the fertility increase, not total births averted, and the value of the result is negative instead of positive.

Now the total net births averted by the program (TNPBA) is divided by TBA* to obtain the proportionate increase in the number of births that would have occurred without the program (PNPBA*). In other words, PNPBA* measures the degree to which the program generated a net fertility reduction, in terms of actual fertility change.

Finally, PNPBA* is multiplied by RA, both of which have negative values in this case, to estimate the net CBR effect of the program (NPE) through its impact on this particular fertility rate. The substantive interpretations of the intermediate calculations in this case are slightly different from interpretations in the preceding two cases, but the interpretation of the final result (NPE) is exactly the same in all three cases since the calculations to derive NPE are identical and because NPE always has a positive value. The mathematical equivalence of the three sets of calculations may be seen by comparing Equations (11) through (14) for the third case with Equations (3) through (6) and Equations (7) through (10).

$$ABA_i = CB_i - AB_i \qquad (11)$$
$$TBA^* = \Sigma ABA_i \qquad (12)$$
$$PNPBA^* = TNPBA/TBA^* \qquad (13)$$
$$NPE = (RA)(PNPBA^*) \qquad (14)$$

This procedure is applicable unless a composition-specific fertility rate is unchanged during the post-implementation period, in which case PNPBA and PNPBA* do not have meaningful values, that is, their value is $\infty$. In the countries studied all composition-specific fertility rates experienced post-implementation change, and this situation does not occur.

Applying these procedures to each composition-specific fertility rate provides several net program effect (NPE) estimates, each of which corresponds to the program influence on the CBR through a particular fertility rate. The final calculations of the second stage of this research design involve summing these NPE estimates to obtain the total percentage of the CBR decline that is a net program effect (TNPE). Subtracting this result from 100 yields the percentage of the CBR decline attributable to indigenous causes (IE). Equations (15) and (16) summarize these last calculations.

$$TNPE = \Sigma NPE \qquad (15)$$
$$IE = 100 - TNPE \qquad (16)$$

## VALIDITY OF THE RESEARCH DESIGN

In terms of the classification system for quasi-experiments developed in Chapter 2, the decomposition analysis—the first stage of this research design—is a one-group pretest-posttest design in which, in the example given, the entire Taiwanese population is the experimental group, and the data for 1964 and 1975 are the pretest and the posttest. Although this genre of quasi-experiment is in general the weakest of those discussed in the critical evaluation, as implemented here the explicit measurement of CBR decline due to age-sex and marital status composition change takes account of these historical/maturational sources of indigenous fertility change.

The analysis of each composition-specific fertility rate—the second stage of the research design—is an interrupted time series quasi-experiment comparing in effect a series of preprogram and postprogram fertility measurements. Since this genre of study is the second strongest discussed in the critical evaluation, the composite design developed here, which combines the pretest-posttest with a set of interrupted time series studies, is one of the most valid implemented to date.

Neither self-selection nor statistical regression biases plague the inferential process of this composite design because the experimental group in each case is the entire population exposed to the family planning program—the entire country. Experimental mortality would undermine particular applications of the design if a country experienced substantial differential net migration during the study period. Fortunately, this does not appear to be the case for any of the countries studied, and bias from experimental mortality is apparently minimal. Instrumentation poses an additional problem if measurement errors exist in the data for the countries studied. This possibility is best evaluated in later chapters which discuss specific countries in detail. The potential validity threat of maturation is eliminated from this research design by the use of extended preprogram fertility time series that allow maturational change after program implementation to be assessed. The longer the preprogram period analyzed, the more effectively the maturational threat is eliminated.

Moreover, to the extent that historical factors produce the same sort of fertility change prior to and following the program, the reasoning that applies to maturation also applies to history. The correctness of the argument clearly depends, however, on the accurate portrayal of preprogram fertility change, that is, the projection assumptions.[2] In describing the nature of fertility declines in developing countries several demographers have noted that these declines have and can be expected to accelerate as time passes. For example, discussing Taiwan, Freedman et al. (1963: 220) state, "The low mortality and the other indicators of social change are all favorable on *a priori* grounds to a decline in fertility. Such a decline appears to have begun and there are indications that it may continue and accelerate." Also regarding Taiwan, Li (1973: 101) concludes from an analysis of the total fertility rate, "This appears to demonstrate that in the absence of a family-planning programme, fertility can decline at a steady and accelerating rate." Kirk (1969: 87) also notes an accelerating preprogram fertility decline in Taiwan.

Discussing first Taiwan and then developing countries more generally, Davis (1967: 735) concludes, "The rapid economic development has been precisely of a type likely to accelerate a drop in reproduction. The rise in manufacturing has been much greater than the rise in either agriculture or construction. The agricultural labor force has thus been squeezed and migration to the cities has skyrocketed. Since housing has not kept pace, urban families have had to restrict reproduction in order to take advantage of career opportunities and avoid domestic inconvenience. Such conditions have historically tended to accelerate a decline in birth rate." Similarly, discussing developing countries in general Hauser (1967: 413) suggests, "It is conceivable that another decade or two of the present type of family planning programs may turn out to have relatively little impact compared with other forces that are accelerating social change in general and, as part of such change, a change in attitudes, values, and behavior in respect to fertility control."

In view of these observations, socioeconomic data for the four countries studied below are assessed to determine the extent to which socioeconomic change occurred and accelerated prior to and following program implementation. Then, given adequate fertility data, if the socioeconomic analysis warrants it, and if fertility change was accelerating prior to the program, projections for analyzing composition-specific fertility rates are derived assuming a continuation of accelerating fertility change during the post-implementation period. These procedures should minimize the biases introduced by historical and maturational forces by attributing most fertility change from these sources to the indigenous fertility decline hypothesis rather than to the program.

Overall, then, this research design is superior to much previous research. Not only are biases due to history and maturation minimized, but, equally important, self-selection and/or statistical regression artifacts that exaggerated any net program effect in most past studies do not plague the present effort.

Before utilizing this design in the case studies of four countries it is necessary to discuss one additional factor that influences the relative validity of the results obtained using this approach. Some instability is present in any time series data, including the time series of composition-specific fertility rates analyzed in this approach. To the extent that a particular time series analyzed here is unstable or erratic, the results of the projection analysis are subject to error. Although the impact of such errors is reduced by the averaging procedures employed in the projections for each case study, the effectiveness of these procedures is inversely related to the magnitude of the instability, that is, the greater the instability, the less effective the averaging procedures are in reducing its impact.

The magnitude of the instability of a particular time series is, in turn, inversely related to the size of the population from which the time series is derived. In the present context this means that, other things equal, a time series of composition-specific fertility rates will be more stable if it is based on and refers to a large population of births and a large population of women than if it refers to a small population of births and a small population of women. The reason is that, other things equal, any particular random exogenous shock will have less impact on a large population than on a small population. Consequently, time series based on large populations will tend to suffer less instability from random exogenous shocks than will those based on small populations.

The implications of this for the results of the present research are the following. First, within a particular country the results from projection analyses of age-specific fertility rates that refer to relatively large numbers of births and/or women will tend to be more valid than the results based on rates that refer to relatively small numbers of births and/or women. Second, the results from projection analyses that estimate the net program effect—through each age group—on the CBR decline will tend to be more valid than the results that estimate the net program effect on a particular age-specific rate, because each such CBR result is obtained from a purely age-specific result by weighting the age-specific result with a factor that takes into account the number of births and the number of women that enter into the calculation of that age-specific rate. Third, the overall results for a country will tend to be more valid than the age-specific results taken individually, because errors in the age-specific results will tend to cancel each other when the age-specific results are summed together. Finally, the results for countries with relatively large populations will tend to be more valid than the results for countries with relatively small popultions. These implications are fundamental to the interpretations of the case studies presented below.

## NOTES

1. As discussed below, the interrupted time series design developed here requires detailed age and marital status specific data. Hence, the secondary criterion used in selecting the four countries studied here was the availability of such data for each.

2. As noted above, though, regardless of the projection assumptions the historical maturational effects of the changing age-sex and marital status compositions are explicitly measured.

# 4

---

# Socioeconomic Change, Demographic Change, and the Family Planning Program in Taiwan

Taiwan is the first country to which the demographic approach developed in Chapter 3 is applied. Taiwan and the other countries studied in Chapters 4 through 7 have been selected for two reasons which were suggested earlier. First, they are all countries which are widely believed to have implemented particularly successful family planning programs. Second, they are all countries for which data are available to implement the research design developed above.

## THE PERIOD OF JAPANESE RULE

Between 1905 and 1945 Taiwan's population doubled to nearly six million, primarily because of its sharply rising rate of natural increase (Figure 3). This rise in natural increase was the result of a decline in the crude death rate from 33.4 to 18.5 due to Japanese mortality reduction efforts following the annexation of Taiwan to the Japanese Empire in 1895.[1] Between 1900 and 1940 the Japanese also promoted economic modernization in Taiwan by expanding irrigation and electrical generating facilities and by extending the operating length of railroads from about 100 to about 900 kilometers. Despite the increased industrial and agricultural output produced by these and other measures, however, the percentage of occupied Taiwanese males employed in agriculture declined only slightly from 69.9 percent to 68.0 percent between 1905 and 1930, and the per capita consumption level of the population remained unchanged.[2]

This stability and the Japanese policy of exercising control in rural areas through the traditional Taiwanese social structure suggest that

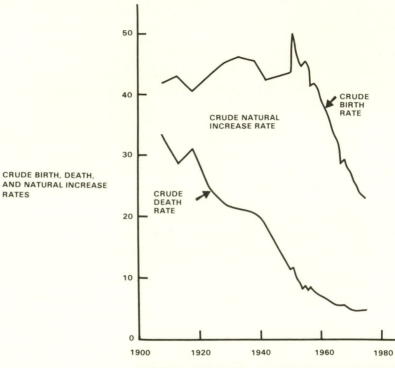

CRUDE BIRTH, DEATH, AND NATURAL INCREASE RATES

SOURCES: BARCLAY, 1954, 241; REPUBLIC OF CHINA, 1973, 1975a

Figure 3. Crude Birth, Death, and Natural Increase Rates for Taiwan Area, 1906–1973

the impact of the Japanese on the social and economic conditions of the Taiwanese population was small. Without much change in social organization the incentive system bearing on reproductive decisions also remains stable, and relatively constant fertility is to be expected. Figure 3 shows that Taiwanese fertility remained high during Japanese rule.

## POSTWAR TAIWAN TO THE FAMILY PLANNING PROGRAM

Less than 20 years after the Japanese departure from Taiwan, accelerated natural increase had combined with immigration to double Taiwan's population to 12 million people. During this period the death rate fell almost without interruption to 5.7 in 1964, while the birth rate first rose to a postwar peak of 50.0 and then fell rapidly to 34.5 in 1964 (Figure 3).

According to several investigators, the profound social and economic transformation of postwar Taiwan accounts for this remarkable fertility decline (Davis, 1967: 734; Freedman et al., 1963: 219–220; and Freedman et al., 1964: 16–17). This transformation intensely affected every major aspect of life. For example, between 1946 and 1964 the proportion of the population 15 years old and above who had achieved at least a junior high school education leaped from less than 1 in 17 to more than 1 in 4, and the proportion of gainfully occupied males working in industries other than agriculture, fishing, and forestry rose from less than one-third to more than one-half (Republic of China, 1975b: 14–17; 1976: 20–23). Residential locations also changed markedly, as the proportion of people living in urban areas increased from about one-half in 1950 to nearly two-thirds in 1964 (Davis, 1967: 735), and the percentage living in large cities of 100,000 or more also increased rapidly from 18.1 percent in 1946 to 29.5 percent in 1964 (Republic of China, 1975b: 12). These and other alterations in Taiwanese society prompted a jump in per capita product of 71 percent between 1951 and 1964 (Republic of China, 1976: 336–339).

The low death rate, the continuing transformation of Taiwanese society, and the declining birth rate led several observers to conclude that a family planning program in Taiwan would face a very favorable situation (Berelson and Freedman, 1964: 29; Freedman et al., 1963: 219–220; and Freedman et al., 1964: 16–17).

## FAMILY PLANNING PROGRAM IMPLEMENTATION

The Taiwanese family planning program was first instituted in the city of Taichung in 1963, and as a result of its apparent success, the Taichung program was expanded to the entire island in 1964 (Freedman and Takeshita, 1969: 15). The 3650 family planning program acceptors of IUDs in 1963 grew to a total of 6178 by the end of the first quarter of 1964. Because this number of acceptors is rather small, and because a birth can be averted by the use of an IUD no sooner than nine months after its adoption, the program could not have significantly affected island-wide fertility before 1965. The number of program acceptors grew rapidly after the first quarter of 1964, however. Therefore, the analysis of Taiwan's fertility decline assumes that the program might have affected fertility during 1965 and later years (for acceptor data see Keeny [1965; 1966], Chow [1974: 108], and Nortman [1971; 1973; 1974; 1975a]).

## DECOMPOSITION OF CRUDE BIRTH RATE DECLINE

The first step in assessing the indigenous and net fertility decline hypotheses is to decompose the CBR decline into three components. Because the Taiwanese program could not have significantly affected fertility until 1965, the CBR for 1964 serves as the preprogram base-line for the decomposition. Between 1964 and 1975 Taiwanese CBR dropped sharply from 34.0 to 23.0.

Since few births in Taiwan are illegitimate, this study assumes all births occur to married women. Given this assumption, the results of the decomposition indicate that about 1 percent of the CBR decline is due to age-sex composition change, assuming the 1964–1975 average of other factors included in the calculations (Table 7).[3] Inspection of the age-specific results shows that this tiny effect is due to much larger but countervailing effects among married women in the quinquennial age groups from 20 to 34.

The tendency toward CBR decline for married women aged 25 to 29 and 30 to 34 resulted from two changes: (1) the percentage of the total population who were women in these age groups declined from 3.5 percent to 3.4 percent for women 25 to 29 and from 3.1 percent to 2.8 percent for women 30 to 34, and (2) the percentage of married people who were married women in these age groups declined from 9.1 percent to 7.7 percent for women 25 to 29 and from 8.4 percent to 7.2 percent for women 30 to 34. Corresponding changes for women aged 20 to 24 tended, overall, to increase rather than decrease the CBR. Combining these countervailing trends with the much smaller effects for other ages shows that about 1 percent of the CBR decline is accounted for by change in the age-sex distribution and is, therefore, attributable to the indigenous fertility decline hypothesis.

An additional 11 percent of the CBR decline can be assigned to marital status composition change, chiefly among women 15 to 19 and 20 to 24. These age-specific effects are due to declines in the percentage of women in each age group who are married, from 10.3 percent to 5.8 percent for women 15 to 19 and from 58.7 percent to 43.2 percent for women 20 to 24. The 15.5 percent reduction for the older women is probably due, at least in part, to a "marriage squeeze." During the later 1960s the age difference between Taiwanese brides and grooms was about five years, but by 1975 women aged 20 to 24 vastly outnumbered men aged 25 to 29 by 836,670 to 576,542 (Chow, 1970: 350; Freedman and Sun, 1969: 17; Republic of China, 1975a: 1128–1139). Since they could not be matched to men of the "proper" marriage age, many of these women may have foregone marriage at least temporarily. Although a potential marriage squeeze also existed for women aged 15 to 19 in 1975 (who outnumbered men aged 20 to 24 by 931,754 to 875,607), these women were probably too young to have felt an effect yet. Looking to the future, girls aged 10 to 14 in 1975 and younger cohorts do not face a marriage squeeze because they are equal or smaller in number than boys five years older.

Marital status composition change among women aged 15 to 24 accounts, overall, for about 14 percent of the CBR decline, but the small countervailing effect among older women reduces the total net effect to about 11 percent. Since both age-sex and marital status composition effects are attributable to the indigenous fertility decline hypothesis, the decomposition shows that 12 percent of the CBR reduction was due to causes other than the family planning program.

The remaining 88 percent of the CBR decline resulted from change in age-sex marital status specific fertility rates. Declining fertility among women aged 25 to 49 was partly offset by increased fertility among younger women to produce the overall effect.

## ANALYSIS OF AGE-SPECIFIC MARITAL FERTILITY RATES

The second step in attributing fertility change to either the indigenous or the net fertility decline hypothesis is the analysis of composition-specific fertility rate changes. Because few illegitimate births occur in Taiwan, the composition-specific fertility rates analyzed are age-specific marital fertility rates—rates that may be calculated for the preprogram period from 1956 to 1964.

These Taiwanese data are of high quality except for the years 1956, when fertility may be overestimated, and 1957, when it may be underestimated. The birth data from which the rates are calculated are obtained from the population registration system. Normally, not all births are reported immediately, and an average time lag exists between the occurrence and the registration of births. On September 16, 1956, however, a census was conducted in Taiwan, and the evidence suggests that people tended to register births more promptly during 1956 than in other years to insure agreement between their registration system information and their census information. Consequently, compared to noncensus years, births were overreported in 1956, and since many births that would normally have been reported during 1957 were instead registered during 1956, the reported number of births during 1957 is underestimated in comparison to other noncensus years. Although published data are corrected for these errors, the corrections are probably not entirely adequate (Republic of China, 1966: 10–13). The same phenomenon also apparently occurred in conjunction with the 1966 census.

Furthermore, all population data are obtained from the registration system except for the years 1956–1958. Population estimates for these years are obtained by linear interpolation and extrapolation from the 1956 census and the 1958 registration data (see Appendix).

In view of these variations in the accuracy and sources of data, projection procedures for analyzing age-specific marital fertility rates are designed to minimize the potential effect of slight errors that may exist. In addition, projection procedures should be chosen to accurately reflect preprogram fertility trends in order to provide valid estimates of program impact. As discussed above, several demographers have noted that fertility declines associated with modernization can be expected to accelerate as time passes. By assessing the pattern of change in age-specific marital fertility rates prior to the program, it can be determined whether preprogram fertility decline was accelerating. To make this assessment in a manner that insures that errors associated with 1956 and 1957 data do not bias conclusions, the mean rates for three sets of dates (1956, 1957, and 1958; 1959, 1960, and 1961; and 1962, 1963, and 1964) are calculated. These means may be interpreted as estimates of fertility for 1957, 1960, and 1963 (Table 8). Using three means allows all available data to be considered and allows any preprogram acceleration in fertility change to be identified, yet minimizes the effects of errors in the data for particular years.

Inferences concerning the nature of preprogram fertility change are drawn from the bottom two lines of Table 8 as follows. For each age group negative numbers indicate decline, positive numbers indicate increase. If, for a specific age group, the two numbers are identical, change is constant. If the absolute value of the more recent figure is larger, then change is accelerating. If, however, the absolute value of the more recent figure is smaller, the change is decelerating.

The large differences between the two bottom rows of Table 8 suggest that none of the women experienced constant fertility change.

**Table 8**
**Estimated Age-Specific Marital Fertility Rates and Fertility Change in Taiwan for 1957, 1960, and 1963**

| Years | Age of Married Woman | | | | | | |
|---|---|---|---|---|---|---|---|
|  | 15-19 | 20-24 | 25-29 | 30-34 | 35-39 | 40-44 | 45-49 |
| Rates | | | | | | | |
| 1957 | 398.2 | 377.6 | 364.8 | 306.0 | 229.8 | 113.4 | 23.3 |
| 1960 | 365.5 | 408.3 | 377.9 | 282.0 | 192.5 | 92.1 | 15.9 |
| 1963 | 362.9 | 427.8 | 379.7 | 246.6 | 149.2 | 68.5 | 11.1 |
| Change | | | | | | | |
| 1957-60 | -32.7 | 30.7 | 13.1 | -24.0 | -37.7 | -21.3 | -7.4 |
| 1960-63 | -2.6 | 19.5 | 1.8 | -35.4 | -43.3 | -23.6 | -4.8 |

Source:  Republic of China, 1956; 1973; 1975a; 1976.

Decelerating fertility decline prior to the program occurred only among women aged 15–19 and 45–49, who together accounted for less than 5 percent of all births in 1964. On the other hand, women aged 30–34, 35–39, and 40–44 (nearly half the age categories) experienced accelerating decline in marital fertility, and women aged 20–24 and 25–29 experienced decelerating increase, a pattern which, if continued, becomes accelerating decline. Hence, the five age groups which accounted for more than 95 percent of all births in 1964 would all have experienced accelerating decline if preprogram trends would have continued.

If fertility change accelerated in response to rapid socioeconomic change prior to the family planning program, then fertility change would be expected to continue into the post-implementation period, even if the program had not been introduced, since socioeconomic change continued unabated. In fact, socioeconomic change itself may have accelerated. Although the percentage of the population with at least a junior high school education rose by approximately the same amount between 1955–1964 and 1964–1973, increases in the level of urbanization, the percentage of males in the nonagricultural labor force, and per capita product were greater during the nine years following the program than during either of the nine year periods for which data are available prior to the program (Republic of China, 1975b: 12–17; 1976: 20–23, 336–339). Fertility projections, therefore, are calculated assuming that accelerating fertility change would have continued beyond 1964 without the introduction of the family planning program.

To accurately reflect the various age-specific patterns of marital fertility change, each set of projected rates for 1965–1975 is calculated by fitting a quadratic equation (second degree polynomial) to the estimated rates reflected in Table 8. Since exactly one quadratic equation can be fitted to a set of three points, the equation derived for each age group is uniquely defined. The quadratic form is chosen because it makes it possible to apply the constant acceleration or deceleration in fertility change observed during the baseline period (1957–1963) in deriving projected fertility rates. In other words, projected fertility rates for Taiwan for the years 1965–1975 are derived on the assumption that accelerations or decelerations in fertility change prior to the program were constant and would have continued in the absence of the program. Because this procedure might in some circumstances lead ultimately to impossible negative rates, it is further assumed that age-specific marital fertility would not have declined below that of the United States in 1973 (U.S. National Center for Health Statistics, 1977). Since the age-specific marital fertility rate for women aged 45–49 is not available for the United States, it is assumed to be one-half the rate for women aged 40 to 44.

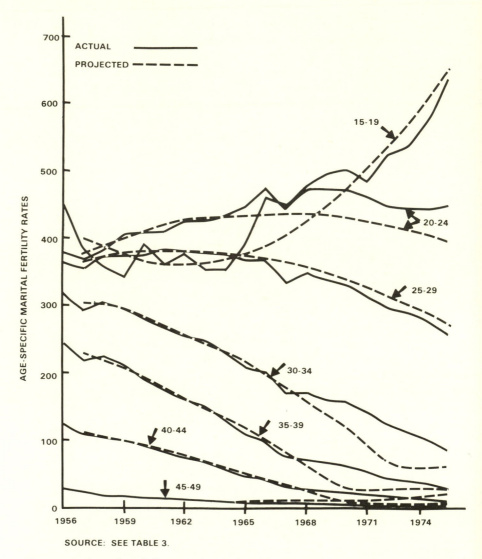

Figure 4. Actual and Projected Age-Specific Marital Fertility Rates for Taiwan, 1956–1975

The actual and the projected rates are depicted in Figure 4. Performing the calculations described above provides estimates of the net program effect on each age-specific marital fertility rate and estimates of the net program effect on the CBR through each age-specific marital fertility rate (Table 9).

The negative seven for women aged 15–19 indicates that their marital fertility would have been 7 percent higher without the program. A large net program effect is found for women aged 25–29 for whom

23 percent of the marital fertility decline is attributed to the program. Among women aged 20–24, 30–34, 35–39, and 40–44, the program effect was small (0–2 percent). Finally, the results indicate that the entire fertility decline of married women aged 45–49 was due to the program and without it their fertility would have increased.

As suggested above, however, the relative validity of these results should be assessed according to the relative number of births and/or women upon which they are based. By this criterion, the results for women aged 45–49 are the least adequate because the number of births occurring to these women between 1956 and 1975 was never as large as 4000 and fell as low as 676, compared to the total number of births which ranged between 365,000 and 425,000. Probably more valid, but

**Table 9**
**Age-Specific Marital Fertility Rate Change and Crude Birth Rate Decline in Taiwan Attributable to Net Program Effect Expressed as Percentages by Age for 1964 to 1975**

| Net program effect on | Age | | | | | | |
|---|---|---|---|---|---|---|---|
| | 15-19 | 20-24 | 25-29 | 30-34 | 35-39 | 40-44 | 45-49 |
| Age-specific marital rate | -7 | 0 | 23 | 2 | 2 | 1 | 151 |
| Crude birth rate | 1 | 0 | 7 | 1 | 0 | 0 | 2 |

Source:  Republic of China, 1956; 1973; 1975a; 1976.

still suspect, are the results for married women aged 15–19 who between 1956 and 1975 never accounted for as much as 4 percent of the married female population aged 15–49. Age-specific results for married women aged 20–44 should be considerably more valid.

The relative magnitude of errors resulting from instability in the time series for the youngest and eldest age groups is reduced when the net program effect for specific age groups is translated into the net program effect, through each group, on the CBR decline because the translation procedure takes account of the numbers of births and women in each age group. In terms of the CBR decline, each age-specific net program effect represents less than 2 percent of the CBR decline, except for the program effect of 7 percent among women aged 25–29.

Taken together, these results imply that the total net program impact was 11 percent of the actual CBR decline. This overall estimate for the entire country should be more reliable than the age-specific results taken individually because errors in the age-specific results will tend to cancel each other when the age-specific results are combined.

## NOTES

1. See Barclay (1954) for a thorough analysis of Japanese colonial activities and population change in Taiwan between 1895 and 1945.

2. Comparable ocupational data for 1931–1943 are not available although somewhat similar data for the entire population suggest the occupational structure of the entire Taiwanese population may have shifted slightly more between 1930 and 1940 (Barclay, 1954: 58).

3. In this table and throughout the monograph, births with an unknown age of mother are distributed proportionally to births with age of mother known.

# 5

# Socioeconomic Change, Demographic Change, and the Family Planning Program in South Korea

## JAPANESE ANNEXATION THROUGH KOREAN WAR

Following its annexation to the Japanese Empire in 1910, Korea's mortality rate declined. Between 1925 and 1945, the earliest period for which fairly reliable data are available, the crude death rate decreased from the upper 20s to the lower 20s. Mortality then stabilized until the 1950–1953 Korean War during which the death rate jumped dramatically. Following the war and into the late 1950s the death rate resumed its prewar decline to 16 in South Korea, considerably below the prewar level. During this period the crude birth rate fluctuated between 40 and 46, reaching a postwar high of about 44. The resulting rate of natural increase grew from roughly 18 in the 1920s to about 28 in the later 1950s (Figure 5).

Despite a Japanese colonial policy of economic modernization in Korea that included agricultural advances and the development of railroads, electricity, and light and heavy manufacturing, the impact on the average Korean was minimal. Educational and economic opportunities for Koreans were limited, their occupational distribution changed little, and per capita food consumption may even have fallen under Japanese rule (Choy, 1971: 166–167; Kuznets, 1977: 17, 87–89). Furthermore, much of the industrial development was concentrated in the northern part of Korea, which was not included within the Republic of Korea following World War II.

Hence, the economic situation of South Korea was precarious during the interwar years, and much of the industrial capacity that did exist was later devastated during the Korean War. The economic

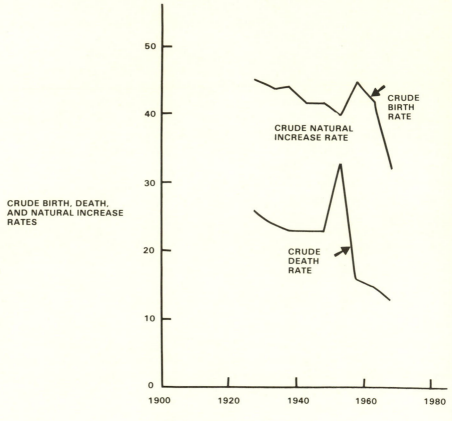

SOURCE: KWON et al. (1975).

Figure 5. Crude Birth, Death, and Natural Increase Rates for All of Korea, 1925–1944, and Republic of Korea, 1955–1970

growth which followed from 1953 to 1958/1959 served largely to merely replace physical capacity lost during the war (Chang, 1966: 210–211; Choy, 1971: 199–201, 345–347; Kuznets, 1977: 40–41). Except for deterioration during the last several years, between 1910 and 1955 the average South Korean's social and economic opportunities changed very little and the reproductive incentive system remained largely intact. This fact is reflected in the birth rate fluctuation around the high, but fairly narrow, range of 40–46 between 1910 and 1955–1960 (Cho, 1973a: 5; Kwon, 1974: 12, 23).

## KOREAN WAR TO FAMILY PLANNING PROGRAM

After the Korean War the long-term mortality decline continued, and a short-lived baby-boom was succeeded by steady fertility decline. Because the birth rate decreased faster than the death rate, natural increase fell from about 28 to 26 between the war's end and the early 1960s (Figure 5). Social and economic change also prevailed during the post Korean War period (Kuznets, 1977: 44, 60; Kwon et al., 1975: 59, 96; and Watson, 1973: 55–61). From 1955 to 1966 the proportion of the population living in cities of 20,000 or more rose from about one in three to more than two in five, with comparable increases for larger cities. School attendance also increased substantially (especially for females) and the percentage of males employed in nonagricultural and nonfishing occupations rose dramatically, from 28 percent to 45 percent in little more than a decade. Per capita consumption also increased, and the per capita gross national product climbed by nearly 1 percent annually between 1953–1955 and 1956–1959 and by more than 5 percent annually from the early to the later 1960s. This socioeconomic transformation continued following the implementation of the family planning program.

## FAMILY PLANNING PROGRAM IMPLEMENTATION

Early in 1963 a "national enlightenment campaign" began in South Korea. Although about 1 million couples registered for family planning services during the campaign, more than 75 percent of them visited health clinics only once to obtain a free one-month supply of condoms or foam tablets. Whether or not these contraceptives were actually used is not known. By the end of 1963 about 1600 women had accepted IUDs and by the end of March 1964 just under 7000 women had accepted them. Thereafter, the nationwide program, which began in May 1964, and the number of acceptors of family planning services grew rapidly (Keeny, 1965: 1–4; 1966: 1–4; Nortman, 1971: 39; 1974: 62). These data suggest that a family planning program effect might have occurred during 1964, but it probably could not have significantly influenced nationwide fertility until 1965.

## DECOMPOSITION OF CRUDE BIRTH RATE DECLINE IN SOUTH KOREA

Since the earliest year that the family planning program could have significantly influenced South Korean fertility is 1965, the ideal baseline year for the decomposition analysis is 1964. In order to minimize the impact of inadequacies in the available data, however, the year centered on January 1, 1963, is chosen as the baseline, and to insure maximum consistency the year centered on January 1, 1971, is employed as the final year of the decomposition (see Appendix). In addition to its purely methodological advantage, the January 1, 1963, baseline also has the advantage of clearly preceding the time when the "national enlightenment campaign" may have affected fertility.

Although the necessary data have not been accurately collected on a continuing basis, two sets of fertility estimates prepared by Cho (1973b: 275) and Moon et al. (1973: 120–123) are combined here with census data to approximate the actual demographic situation in South Korea during the period of interest. As with Taiwan, since few births in South Korea are illegitimate, the present study assumes all births occur to married women (a more detailed explanation of the procedures used is presented in the Appendix). Estimates based on Cho's data imply a CBR decline from 38.9 to 28.1 between 1963 and 1971, while corresponding estimates based on Moon's data imply a decline from 40.0 to 30.7. These estimates suggest South Korea's fertility declined dramatically during the short eight-year period. The decompositions of these CBR declines indicate that between 23 percent and 25 percent resulted from age-sex composition change and between 20 percent and 23 percent resulted from marital composition change (Table 10).

The age-specific results based on the two sets of fertility estimates, which are also fairly similar, show that the age-sex effect is dominated by women aged 20–24 and 25–29. Large effects occur for these women because (1) the percentage of the population in these age groups fell from 4.2 percent to 3.9 percent for the younger ages and from 3.9 percent to 3.5 percent for the older group, and (2) the percentage of married people who were married women in these ages fell from 6.9 percent to 4.8 percent for the younger group and from 10.1 percent to 9.0 percent for the older group. Although the corresponding changes for women aged 30–44 were in the opposite direction, the magnitude was much less. Consequently, between 23 percent and 25 percent of the CBR decline resulted, overall, from age-sex composition change.

Nearly as large, the 20 percent to 23 percent marital status effect results from two major changes. First, underlying each age-specific marital status effect is the drop in the percentage of the total population that is married from 35.6 percent to 34.4 percent. Second, the largest age-specific effect, which accounts for roughly two-thirds of the total effect, occurred mainly because the percentage of women aged 20–24 who were married decreased from 58.7 percent to 42.0 percent. Both of these changes in the marital status distribution were continuations of secular trends that began around 1930.

These changes in the population composition, which altogether account for nearly one-half of the 1963–1971 South Korean CBR decline, are attributable to indigenous causes that are entirely independent of the family planning program. The remaining CBR decline is

**Table 10**
**Decomposition of Crude Birth Rate Decline in South Korea**
**Expressed as Percentages by Age for January 1, 1963, to January 1,**
**1971**

| Percent of decline due to | All ages | Age of married woman | | | | | |
| --- | --- | --- | --- | --- | --- | --- | --- |
| | | 15-19 | 20-24 | 25-29 | 30-34 | 35-39 | 40-44 |
| Age-sex effect | 23[a] | 2[a] | 16[a] | 13[a] | -4[a] | -3[a] | -1[a] |
| | 25[b] | 1[b] | 19[b] | 15[b] | -5[b] | -4[b] | -1[b] |
| Marital status effect | 20[a] | 2[a] | 14[a] | 3[a] | 1[a] | 0[a] | 0[a] |
| | 23[b] | 2[b] | 16[b] | 4[b] | 1[b] | 0[b] | 0[b] |
| Rate effect | 57[a] | 1[a] | -5[a] | 5[a] | 24[a] | 21[a] | 11[a] |
| | 52[b] | 1[b] | -10[b] | -5[b] | 23[b] | 30[b] | 13[b] |
| Total | 100[a] | 5[a] | 25[a] | 21[a] | 21[a] | 18[a] | 10[a] |
| | 100[b] | 4[b] | 25[b] | 14[b] | 19[b] | 26[b] | 12[b] |

[a]Based on Cho's fertility estimates

[b]Based on 1971 Fertility-Abortion Survey

Source:  Cho, 1973b; Moon et al. 1973; Republic of Korea, 1960; 1966; 1970.

due to variation in age-specific marital fertility rates, which requires further analysis.

## ANALYSIS OF AGE-SPECIFIC MARITAL FERTILITY RATES

By projecting preprogram change into later years and comparing the projections with actual post-implementation fertility, composition-specific fertility rate change is assigned either to the family planning program or to indigenous causes. To minimize the impact of various sources of error in the South Korean data, estimated composition-specific fertility rates are calculated for January 1, 1961, and January 1, 1964, and projected assuming linear change to obtain expected rates for 1966 through 1971 (see Appendix). Since illegitimate fertility is slight in South Korea, only age-specific marital fertility rates for women are analyzed. Although available data are somewhat unreliable, the calculation of estimates based on both Cho (1973b) and Moon et al.

(1973) data provides a range of values within which the actual indigenous and program effects probably lie.

After implementation of the family planning program, social and economic modernization initiated between the Korean War and the program continued (Kwon et al., 1975: 59, 96; Kuznets, 1977: 44, 60; Watson, 1973: 55–61). Moreover, according to certain indicators of modernization, such as the level of urbanization and per capita production and consumption, the pace of modernization accelerated. Consequently, even if the program had not been instituted, the substantial age-specific marital fertility reductions between 1961 and 1964 would be expected to continue (Figures 6 and 7).

To minimize the effect of imperfect data, projections are derived with the simple assumption that preprogram fertility change was linear and postprogram change would have continued in a linear fashion had the program not been implemented. It is assumed further that fertility would not have fallen below that of the United States in 1973. The resulting estimates based on Cho's data imply that the program had no net effect on women aged 15–34, but that it did produce about 4 percent of the marital fertility decline among women aged 35–39 and about 2 percent of the decline among women aged 40–44. These are rather small effects.

For women aged 15–19 the results based on Moon's data are, however, quite different, indicating a net program effect of 91 percent instead of 0 percent. This difference appears to be due to instability in the fertility trends, as estimated by Cho and Moon et al., resulting from the relatively tiny number of births and women that enter into the calculation of these rates. Married women aged 15–19 account for less than 4 percent of all married women aged 15–44 and less than 2.5 percent of all births in South Korea during this period. As discussed above, net program effect estimates on the fertility of such an age group should be considerably less valid than estimates of the net program effect on the CBR decline through the age group because the CBR decline estimates take into account the relative size and number of births occurring to the group. This expectation appears to be borne out in Table 11. The CBR decline estimates for married women aged 15–19 differ by less than one-half of 1 percent.

The net program effect estimates on age-specific rates that are derived for groups that include relatively large numbers of women and who experience relatively large numbers of births should be considerably more valid. This also appears to be the case. For women aged 20–24 and 25–29 the estimates based on the Cho data and the Moon et al. data are identical, and for women aged 35–39 and 40–44 the estimates are reasonably close. The age-specific estimates of net program effects on the CBR decline should be still more valid. This ex-

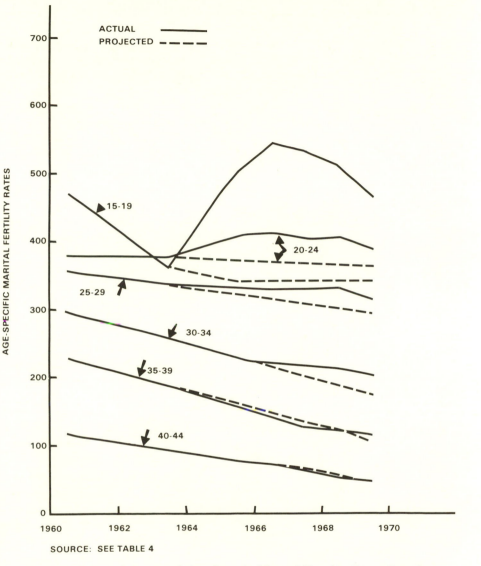

SOURCE: SEE TABLE 4

Figure 6. Actual and Projected Age-Specific Marital Fertility Rates Based on
Cho (1973b) Data for South Korea, January 1, 1961, to January 1, 1970

pectation is supported; for women aged 20–24, 25–29, 35–39, and 40–
44 the differences between the estimates based on the Cho data and
the Moon et al. data lie within the narrow range of 0 percent to 2 percent. For women aged 30–34 the difference in the age-specific rate effect estimates is substantially larger (31 percent) but taking into account the relative size and number of births to this group in the CBR

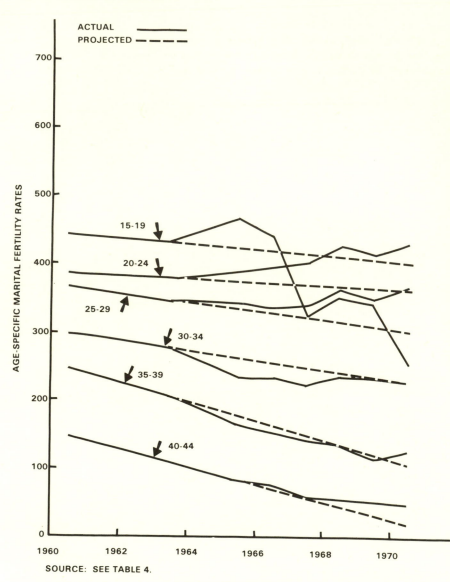

Figure 7. Actual and Projected Age-Specific Marital Fertility Rates Based on Moon et al. (1973) Data for South Korea, January 1, 1961, to January 1, 1971

decline estimate reduces the difference to 7 percent. This discrepancy is probably due to inadequacies in the basic data from which Cho and Moon et al. derive their estimates and to differences in the procedures they employ.

Finally, the most valid results should be the estimates for the entire country. The two estimates of the net program effect, based on

**Table 11**
**Age-Specific Marital Fertility Rate Change and Crude Birth Rate Decline in South Korea Attributable to Net Program Effect Expressed as Percentages by Age for January 1, 1965, to January 1, 1971**

| Net program effect on | Age | | | | | |
|---|---|---|---|---|---|---|
| | 15-19 | 20-24 | 25-29 | 30-34 | 35-39 | 40-44 |
| Age-specific marital rate | 0[a] | 0[a] | 0[a] | 0[a] | 4[a] | 2[a] |
| Crude birth rate | 0[a] | 0[a] | 0[a] | 0[a] | 1[a] | 0[a] |
| Age-specific marital rate | 91[b] | 0[b] | 0[b] | 31[b] | 10[b] | 1[b] |
| Crude birth rate | 0[b] | 0[b] | 0[b] | 7[b] | 3[b] | 0[b] |

[a]Based on Cho's fertility estimates

[b]Based on 1971 Fertility-Abortion Survey

Source: Cho, 1973b; Moon et al. 1973; Republic of Korea, 1960; 1966; 1970.

the work of Cho and Moon et al., lie within the fairly narrow range of 1 percent to 10 percent of the CBR decline between 1964 and 1971. This represents a reduction in the CBR of between 0.1 and 1.0 point. The remaining 90 percent to 99 percent of the decline can be attributed to indigenous causes.

## CONCLUSIONS

An analysis of the relative validity of the results for South Korea and for Taiwan suggests that they may be roughly comparable. On one hand, one would expect the results for South Korea to be more valid, other things equal, because its population is approximately twice the size of Taiwan's, and hence the trends upon which the projections of this study depend should be more stable. On the other hand, the basic data for Taiwan are considerably better than the data for South Korea, and the preprogram period analyzed for Taiwan is much longer. These factors tend to offset each other, and it is interesting to note that the overall net program effect estimates are roughly the same for the two countries, 11 percent for Taiwan and 1–10 percent for South Korea.

# 6

---

# Socioeconomic Change, Demographic Change, and the Family Planning Program in Costa Rica

## PREPROGRAM PERIOD

Throughout the twentieth century Costa Rica's population has grown rapidly. With less than one-quarter of a million people in 1892 the population nearly doubled by 1927, and almost tripled to 1.3 million in 1963. Natural increase accounts for most of this growth.

Beginning at the substantial level of 1.7 percent per year in 1910–1919, the rate of natural increase more than doubled by 1960 to a remarkable 3.9 percent in 1960. Dominating this dramatic rise was a 20 point drop in the crude death rate from 29.8 to 9.3. The CBR during this period fluctuated within the narrow but high range of 44 to 49, first falling slowly through the 1940s, then rising more rapidly through 1959. The next decade brought a slight death rate reduction which contrasted sharply with the precipitous drop in the birth rate (Figure 8, Gomez and Bermudez, 1974: 3; Gomez and Reynolds, 1973: 319).

The slight birth rate change prior to 1959 accompanied gradual, but quite limited, socioeconomic modernization (Republica de Costa Rica, 1953; 1966; 1974). By 1950 only one-fifth of the people aged 15–54 had completed primary school and less than one in twenty had completed secondary school. Similarly, about two-thirds of the economically active males were engaged in farming, fishing, lumbering and related occupations. In addition, two-thirds of the total population lived in rural areas.

Between 1950 and 1963 socioeconomic change apparently accelerated as people aged 15–34 experienced an especially rapid educa-

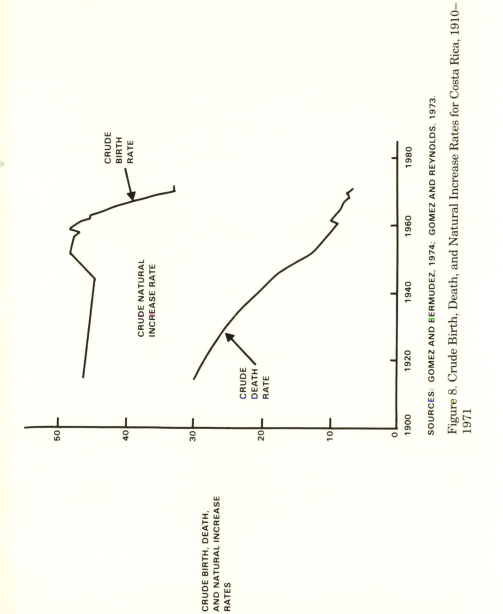

CRUDE BIRTH, DEATH, AND NATURAL INCREASE RATES

SOURCES: GOMEZ AND BERMUDEZ, 1974; GOMEZ AND REYNOLDS, 1973.

Figure 8. Crude Birth, Death, and Natural Increase Rates for Costa Rica, 1910–1971

tional advance. The percentage who completed at least primary school jumped from about 20 percent to between 28 percent and 42 percent for different ages. Smaller, but notable, gains also occurred for people aged 35–54. The proportion achieving a secondary education also increased. During the same period the percentage of males in primary economic activities decreased from 64 percent to 56 percent and urbanization increased somewhat (see Gomez and Bermudez [1974: 3–4] and English [1971: 111–112] for limitations of the urban and rural definitions in Costa Rica). This socioeconomic change, particularly the accelerated rise in education among those in their first 20 reproductive years, is apparently the underlying factor in the sudden fertility decline that began in 1960.

## FAMILY PLANNING PROGRAM IMPLEMENTATION

Although a limited family planning program was established in Costa Rica during 1962, the national program was not instituted until 1967. The estimated number of *current* family planning program users was quite small through 1964, but grew steadily during succeeding years. The first year that at least 1 percent of women aged 15–49 were current users of program-supplied contraception was 1967 (Reynolds, 1973: 315). Therefore, this research assumes that the program could not have significantly affected fertility until 1968.

## DECOMPOSITION OF CRUDE BIRTH RATE DECLINE

Because the family planning program probably could not have significantly affected nationwide fertility in Costa Rica until 1968, the baseline year for the decomposition is 1967. The final year employed is 1971, the most recent year for which a continuously reliable time series of data is available.

Unlike the Taiwanese and South Koreans who can readily be identified as married or unmarried, many Costa Ricans live in a third, intermediate marital status—consensual unions. Women in each marital status category probably differ in many regards, most notably for present purposes in their frequency of sexual intercourse. Any differences, therefore, in the fertility levels and rates of change among women in each marital status will combine with change in the distribution of women in each status to influence overall fertility. Ideally, data specific to each of the three marital statuses would be employed in the decomposition in order to estimate birth rate change from each of these possible sources. Unfortunately, birth data for each marital status by age are not available. In lieu of such data, this research treats women living in consensual unions as married, and assumes all births occur to them, while women outside such unions are considered unmarried with no fertility.

Although these data and assumptions reduce the specificity of conclusions drawn, the more general inferences that can be drawn should be quite accurate for two reasons. First, women who are *not* living in marital or consensual unions probably experience infrequent sexual intercourse and slight fertility compared to women within such unions who, presumably, are regularly exposed to intercourse and the risk of pregnancy. Assuming this is true, the marital status and fertility assumptions should produce fairly accurate results. Second, the ratio of

**Table 12**
**Decomposition of Crude Birth Rate Decline in Costa Rica Expressed as Percentages by Age for 1967 to 1971**

| Percent of decline due to | Age of married woman | | | | | | | |
|---|---|---|---|---|---|---|---|---|
| | All ages | 15-19 | 20-24 | 25-29 | 30-34 | 35-39 | 40-44 | 45-49 |
| Age-sex effect | -4 | -4 | -4 | 0 | 3 | 1 | 0 | 0 |
| Marital status effect | -3 | 0 | 0 | -1 | -1 | -1 | 0 | 0 |
| Rate effect | 107 | 2 | 22 | 31 | 23 | 23 | 5 | 1 |
| Total | 100 | -2 | 18 | 30 | 25 | 23 | 5 | 1 |

Source: Gomez and Reynolds, 1973; Republica de Costa Rica, 1953; 1966; 1974.

women in consensual unions to women in formal marriages changed little during the period studied. Hence, regardless of any fertility differential between them, the small change in the distribution of women in each category will influence their overall fertility little (Republica de Costa Rica, 1953; 1966; 1974).

Between 1967 and 1971 the Costa Rican CBR fell 18 percent from 40.2 to 33.1 (see Appendix). The decomposition of this decline shows that, assuming the 1967–1971 average of other factors, both the age-sex and the marital status compositions tended to produce CBR increase (Table 12). Women aged 15–24 account for most of the slight age-sex effect because the percentage of the population in these ages increased, from 5.5 percent to 5.8 percent for 15–19 year-olds and from 4.3 percent to 4.5 percent for 20–24 year-olds, and because the percentage of married people who were married women aged 15–19 increased from 2.8 percent to 2.9 percent. The effects were only partly counteracted by corresponding decreases for women aged 30–39. The smaller tendency for change in the marital status composition to produce birth rate rise is mainly accounted for by women aged 25–39. This occurred because the married population increased from 29.6 percent to 30.1 percent of the total population and because of age-specific increases in the percentage married, from 77.3 percent to 77.6 percent for women aged 30–34 and from 77.9 percent to 78.7 percent for women aged 35–39.

The age-sex and marital status effects are overwhelmed by age-specific marital fertility declines. These declines occurred at all ages and completely counteracted the preceding effects for each age group except the youngest. Most of the birth rate decline is accounted for by fertility declines among married women aged 20–39 (Table 12).

## ANALYSIS OF AGE-SPECIFIC MARITAL FERTILITY RATES

Age-specific marital fertility in Costa Rica began a long-term descent in either 1960 or 1961 for women of all ages except those aged 40–44 whose fertility began to decline in 1962 (Figure 9). It seems likely that this fall in marital fertility was a response to the apparent acceleration in socioeconomic change noted above, an acceleration that may have begun about 1950.

According to several indicators, the pace of socioeconomic change accelerated again after 1963 (Republica de Costa Rica, 1953; 1966; 1974). The percentage of people aged 15–54 who had achieved at least a primary education rose 10 percent during the 13 years that preceded 1963, but then jumped dramatically by 20 percent during the next 10 years. The acceleration in the rising percentage of people attaining at least a secondary education was also remarkable, especially for women who tripled their 1950–1963 increase to 6 percent in the decade after 1963.

Corresponding shifts occurred in the occupational distribution, where the 8 percent 13-year rise in the percentage of men in nonprimary occupations jumped to a 12 percent 10-year rise. Similar changes occurred in the percent urban, although definitional problems undermine the data. In addition, the fluctuating but relatively constant per capita energy consumption between 1950 and 1961 was followed in 1962 by an unprecedented level of consumption, and by a rapid and nearly uninterrupted rise in consumption that accelerated as time passed (United Nations, 1976b: 53). Finally, a decade of near stagnation in per capita GNP was followed by a rapid increase after 1964 (Wilkie, 1976: 231).

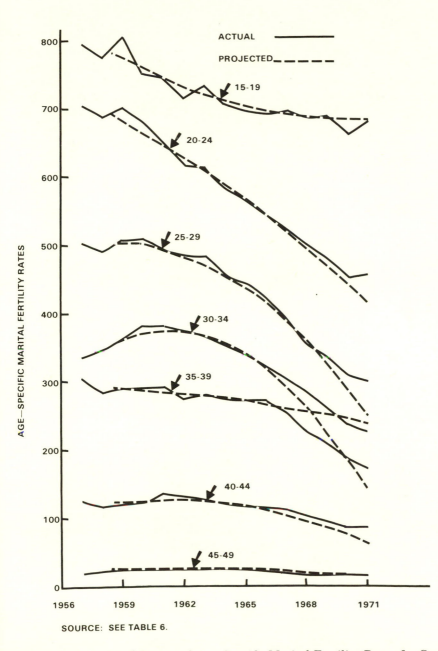

ACTUAL ⎯⎯⎯⎯⎯
PROJECTED ⎯ ⎯ ⎯ ⎯

15-19
20-24
25-29
30-34
35-39
40-44
45-49

AGE—SPECIFIC MARITAL FERTILITY RATES

800
700
600
500
400
300
200
100
0

1956   1959   1962   1965   1968   1971

SOURCE: SEE TABLE 6.

Figure 9. Actual and Projected Age-Specific Marital Fertility Rates for Costa Rica, 1957–1971

Given the apparently increasing rate of socioeconomic change after 1960, accelerating fertility decline seems likely and is assumed in the last stage of this case study. Specifically, postprogram projections of marital fertility are derived as follows. First, for each five-year age group, preprogram marital fertility rates are derived for three dates: fertility for the year centered on January 1, 1959, is derived as the mean of fertility for 1957, 1958, 1959, and 1960; fertility for the year centered on July 1, 1962, is derived as the mean of fertility for 1960, 1961, 1962, 1963, and 1964; and for the year centered on January 1, 1966, fertility is derived as the mean of fertility for 1964, 1965, 1966, and 1967. Although this procedure, which is similar to that employed for Taiwan and South Korea, is designed both to allow the use of all

**Table 13**
**Age-Specific Marital Fertility Rate Change and Crude Birth Rate Decline in Costa Rica Attributable to Net Program Effect Expressed as Percentages by Age for 1967 to 1971**

| Net program effect on | Age | | | | | | |
|---|---|---|---|---|---|---|---|
| | 15-19 | 20-24 | 25-29 | 30-34 | 35-39 | 40-44 | 45-49 |
| Age-specific marital rate | 43 | 0 | 2 | 0 | 87 | 0 | 76 |
| Crude birth rate | 1 | 0 | 1 | 0 | 20 | 0 | 1 |

Source:  Gomez and Reynolds, 1973; Republica de Costa Rica, 1953; 1966; 1974.

the available data and to provide relatively stable estimates by minimizing the influence of random fluctuation in fertility, the results are likely to be less valid than the results for Taiwan and South Korea because the population of Costa Rica is much smaller. Taiwan has approximately 8 times as many people and South Korea has approximately 15 times as many people as Costa Rica. The results for Costa Rica are presented in Table 13.

Among the various age groups in Costa Rica, the estimated net program effects for married women aged 15–19 and 45–49 are most likely to suffer from instability. Married women aged 15–19 account for a smaller proportion of married women aged 15–49 than any other five-year age group, and married women aged 45–49 account for the second smallest proportion and also account for less than 1 percent of all births. The apparent effect of the resulting instability in the estimates for these women is reflected in the very large difference between the magnitudes of estimates of the net program effects on their marital fertility compared to the size of the effects for most other age groups. When these results are translated into estimates of the net program effect on the CBR, a procedure that takes account of the number of births and women in each age group, the results for these women are quite similar to the results for women in most other age groups.

Among the remaining five age groups, only for married women aged 35–39 is the net program effect greater than 2 percent of the marital fertility change and greater than 1 percent of the CBR decline. For women aged 35–39 the estimated effects are 87 percent and 20 percent. An inspection of the actual and projected postprogram changes suggests that this anomaly may be due to the relatively small size of the Costa Rican population. Specifically, married women aged 35–39 experienced a fertility decline much sharper than the projected decline, but the experience of women aged 30–34 presents nearly a mirror image. Their fertility declined much more slowly than the projected decline. In fact by 1971 the value of the projected rate for each group is fairly close to the actual value for the other group (Figure 9).

On the hypothesis that this rather striking result is due to the small population sizes involved, the two sets of birth and population data have been combined, and the procedures that were applied to the five-year age groups have been applied to the new ten-year age group. The result is that actual and projected postprogram fertility correspond closely—the projected value is within 7 percent of the actual value for every postprogram year. The new estimate of the net program effect on the age-specific marital fertility rate of women aged 30–39 is 3 percent, and the new estimate of the effect on the CBR is 1 percent. These results are comparable in magnitude to the results for most other ages. Nevertheless, compared to the results for Taiwan and South Korea, these are somewhat suspect.

The overall results for the country are probably more valid than the age-specific results for reasons discussed above. The results in Table 13 can be combined to derive an estimated net program effect of 23 percent of the CBR decline. Alternatively, the results for the ten-year age group 30–39 can be combined with those for the other five-year age groups to derive an estimated net program effect of 4 percent.

## CONCLUSIONS

Perhaps the most valid conclusion that can be drawn from these calculations is that the actual net program effect probably lies somewhere between 4 percent and 23 percent of the CBR decline, but probably closer to 4 percent. Although this result is somewhat inexact compared to the results for Taiwan and South Korea, the difference in the degree of certainty appears to be warranted by the relatively small size of the Costa Rican population and the concomitant instability in the fertility trends.

# 7

# Socioeconomic Change, Demographic Change, and the Family Planning Program in Mauritius

## PREPROGRAM PERIOD

The population of Mauritius, a tiny island in the Indian Ocean, grew slowly from the turn of the century through World War II, but then increased spectacularly. Although the population of 419,185 in 1944 was only 13 percent larger than it had been 43 years earlier, during the next 18 years the population expanded by 63 percent to 681,619 (Mauritius, 1972).

This pattern resulted mainly from change in the rate of natural increase. Between 1871 and 1946 natural increase or decrease seldom exceeded 1 percent as the crude birth and death rates fluctuated around high levels (Figure 10). During the early twentieth century the death rate typically surpassed 30 and the birth rate typically exceeded 35. Between 1925 and 1946, however, the death rate fell to the high 20s and the birth rate declined to the low 30s (Brookfield [1957: 104–107]; Titmuss and Abel-Smith [1968: 47–51]; and Toussaint [1973: 103–104] discuss these fluctuations and probable causes).

Although malaria deaths reached a peak in 1946, a thorough anti-malaria campaign virtually eliminated such deaths by 1952 and the death rate dropped sharply from 29 to 15 (Brookfield, 1957; Toussaint, 1973: 116). This mortality reduction combined with a somewhat smaller rise in the birth rate, producing a spectacular leap in the rate of natural increase from 0.9 percent in 1946 to 3.5 percent in 1950. Then the death rate decline continued, although more slowly, and the birth rate began a long-term descent.

According to most indicators, these postwar demographic changes

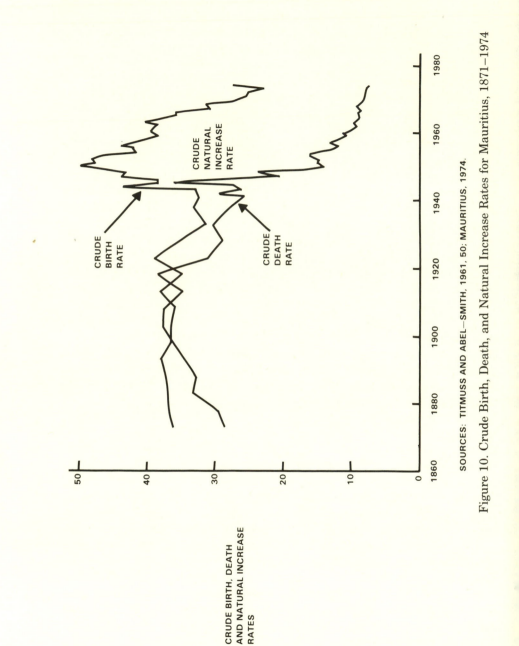

Figure 10. Crude Birth, Death, and Natural Increase Rates for Mauritius, 1871–1974

accompanied socioeconomic modernization. Between 1948 and 1952 the per capita Gross National Product (GNP) grew by 49 percent, and between 1952 and 1968 total GNP increased by nearly 60 percent. Despite the economic expansion during the second period, however, no per capita gains occurred because the population increased at roughly the same pace (Xenos, 1970: 4). Nevertheless, socioeconomic change was evident (Mauritius, 1953; 1962; United Nations, 1976b: 29). For example, the single most important industry on the island—sugar—underwent considerable modernization (Meade et al., 1968: 74–75; Ramdin, 1969: 23, 26). The occupational distribution of economically active males also shifted after 1952 as the percentage of males with occupations other than farming, fishing, hunting, and lumbering surpassed 60 percent. Socioeconomic modernization between 1952 and 1962 is also reflected in the 82 percent increase in total energy consumption, and the 18 percent rise in per capita energy consumption.

The most dramatic manifestation of socioeconomic change, however, is the sharp jump in educational attainment. Overall, the percentage of males attaining at least one year of primary education rose from 63 percent to 76 percent during the decade, and for females the percentage increased from 43 percent to 60 percent. Moreover, the percentage attaining at least some education beyond the primary years roughly doubled during the decade. These rising educational levels reflect rising aspirations for upward social and economic mobility, which provide an escape from mainly agricultural, manual labor to occupations emphasizing intellectual activity. The rather limited opportunities for upward mobility, suggested by the lack of per capita GNP growth between 1952 and 1968 and the relatively slow shift in the occupational distribution, evidently merged with rising educational and occupational aspirations to intensify the competition for existing opportunities.[1] The simultaneous birth rate decline from 49.7 in 1950 to 35.7 in 1965 suggests that this emerging socioeconomic milieu fostered corresponding change in the reproductive incentive system.

The distribution of people in urban and rural places may also have changed, although estimates vary considerably.[2] In any event, the distinction between rural and urban residence is slight in Mauritius compared to most other third world countries because of its small size and good communications. The 720 square-mile island is less than 40 miles long and 30 miles wide, and no point on the island is more than 25 miles from the nearest town (Wright, 1974: 11; Xenos, 1970: 3). With over 600 miles of well-surfaced roads, no spot on the island is more than seven or eight miles from a main road, and the more than 20,000 vehicles and the frequent bus service provide easy access to urban areas (Ramdin, 1969: 41; Benedict, 1965: 23). Finally, little subsistence agriculture exists and nearly the entire population is tied to the cash economy (Benedict, 1965: 8; Brookfield, 1957: 114). Consequently, any rural-urban differential in fertility was virtually eliminated by 1953 (Brookfield, 1957: 108).

Hence, the small size of Mauritius and the ease of transportation, together with the nature of its occupational distribution and sharply rising educational levels, belie the classification of the majority of the population as rural. Instead they reflect the more urban character of Mauritius. Faced with this increasingly pervasive urban environment, many in Mauritius apparently hoped to fulfill surging occupational aspirations for themselves and their children through educational advance, only to be thwarted by slow economic growth and minor shifts in the occupational structure. The dramatic drop in the birth rate during this period suggests that many chose to forego large numbers of children in order to maximize the resources available to existing family members in their quest for a higher social status and standard of living.

## FAMILY PLANNING PROGRAM IMPLEMENTATION

The first year that the family planning program of Mauritius attracted a significant number of acceptors is 1964, but only 73 of the 894 acceptors chose a method other than the rhythm method (Xenos, 1970: 6–9). Therefore, the program could not have significantly affected fertility during 1965. Because the number of acceptors and particularly the number of acceptors of methods other than the rhythm method grew rapidly during the ensuing years, this study assumes that the program might have influenced fertility during 1966 and beyond (Nortman, 1971: 39; 1975a: 59).

## DECOMPOSITION OF CRUDE BIRTH RATE DECLINE

The baseline year for the decomposition of the CBR of Mauritius is 1965 since this is the most recent year that the program could not have affected fertility. The final year employed is 1975.

The derivation of decomposition results for Mauritius depends on surmounting the same obstacles that impeded the analysis for Costa Rica. As in Costa Rica, a substantial proportion of the women in Mauritius live in consensual unions, as opposed to legally or religiously sanctified marriages. Also as in the case of Costa Rica, birth data for women in consensual unions are not collected and reported separately. Consequently, the decomposition is calculated with the same assumptions used for Costa Rica—women in consensual unions are considered married and all births are attributed to consensually, legally, or religiously married women, but none are attributed to other women. Because the percentage of these "married" women who are partners in consensual unions changed little during the period studied, the decomposition results should be minimally biased (Mauritius, 1953; 1962; 1972).

Between 1965 and 1975 the crude birth rate of Mauritius fell from 36.2 to 24.7. Decomposing this reduction shows that change in the age-sex composition tended to produce CBR increase, assuming the 1965–1975 average of other factors considered (Table 14). This slight effect was due mainly to countervailing trends among women aged 20–24

**Table 14**
**Decomposition of Crude Birth Rate Decline in Mauritius, Married Includes Legally and Religiously Married and Partners in Consensual Unions, Expressed as Percentages by Age for 1965 to 1975**

| Percent of decline due to | Age of married woman | | | | | | | |
|---|---|---|---|---|---|---|---|---|
| | All ages | 15-19 | 20-24 | 25-29 | 30-34 | 35-39 | 40-44 | 45-49 |
| Age-sex effect | -1 | 4 | -13 | 1 | 3 | 4 | 0 | 0 |
| Marital status effect | 33 | 15 | 13 | 4 | 1 | 0 | 0 | 0 |
| Rate effect | 68 | -9 | 15 | 15 | 21 | 18 | 7 | 1 |
| Total | 100 | 10 | 15 | 20 | 25 | 22 | 7 | 1 |

Source: Mauritius, 1962; 1972; United Nations, 1970; 1976a.

and women aged 15–19 and 30–39. For women aged 20–24 the strong tendency to produce a rising birth rate was due to two changes during 1965–1975: (1) the percentage of the population that was women aged 20–24 increased from 7.3 percent to 7.6 percent reflecting the postwar baby-boom, and (2) the percentage of married people who were married women aged 20–24 increased from 3.9 percent to 5.1 percent. This effect was nearly eliminated by opposing changes of a similar nature for women of most other ages.

In striking contrast, nearly one-third of the CBR reduction resulted from change in the marital status distribution, especially for women aged 15–29. The decline attributable to these women is due to a fall in the percentage of the total population that was married from 32.8 percent to 31.6 percent, as well as to reductions in the percentage of women in each group who were married, from 21.5 percent to 9.9 percent for women aged 15–19, from 60.5 percent to 46.8 percent for women aged 20–24, and from 80.7 percent to 74.4 percent for women aged 25–29.

Combining the opposing effects of change in the age-sex and marital status distributions shows that about one-third of the 1965–1975 CBR decline is attributable to the indigenous fertility decline hypothesis. The remaining two-thirds of the CBR reduction, which is due to marital fertility declines among women aged 20–44 (Table 14), requires further analysis.

## ANALYSIS OF AGE-SPECIFIC MARITAL FERTILITY RATES

An overview of postwar fertility change in Mauritius, as shown in Figure 10, indicates that the birth rate peak in 1950 preceded a long-term secular decline. Although the preprogram decline temporarily paused to produce minor peaks in 1952, 1956, 1961, and 1963, the long-term trend was downward, as the birth rate fell substantially from 49.7 in 1950 to 35.7 in 1965.

The social and economic transformation that apparently generated this preprogram decline continued after the program was implemented in 1965 (Mauritius, 1953; 1962; 1972; United Nations, 1976b: 29). For example, the percentage of economically active males working in occupations other than farming, fishing, hunting, and lumbering rose from 63 percent in 1962 to 69 percent in 1972. Moreover, between 1952–1962 and 1962–1972, the increases in both total and per capita energy consumption accelerated.

Perhaps most significant for Mauritius is the fact that increases in the percentages of men and women achieving at least some primary education and achieving at least some education beyond the primary level continued and apparently accelerated for at least some ages. By 1972, therefore, the percentage of men with some primary education probably ranged from 67 percent for ages 45–54 to about 90 percent for ages 20–24, and for women the corresponding range was probably from 41 percent to about 80 percent. Similarly, the percentages in 1972 for those obtaining at least some post-primary education probably ranged from 8 percent for men and 5 percent for women aged 45–54 to 27 percent for men and 15 percent for women aged 25–34.

Since, according to these indicators, socioeconomic modernization continued and in some cases accelerated during the post-implementation period, continued birth rate decline should have occurred after 1965, even without the family planning program. This conclusion is further supported by the rise in abortions, despite their illegality. "Thus, in 1959, 774 cases with complications following abortion were admitted to hospitals, representing one abortion for about 31 live births; while in 1969, 2,837 such cases were admitted representing one abortion for about 8 live births, the proportion having almost steadily increased over the ten-year period" (Xenos, 1970: 7). Moreover, if the family planning program had not been instituted and had not provided contraception that might substitute for abortions, abortions might have increased more rapidly.

Despite the considerable likelihood that fertility would have continued to decline after 1965 even in the absence of the program, the derivation of marital fertility projections that reflect this expectation faces a serious obstacle. A casual inspection of the marital fertility trends in Figure 11 indicates that, compared to most of the corresponding trends for Taiwan, South Korea, and Costa Rica, the trends for Mauritius are rather erratic. This is not surprising since the populations of these countries exceed the population of Mauritius by factors ranging from 2 to 30, but the unfortunate consequence is that the projection procedures of this study are somewhat difficult to apply and the results obtained are relatively less valid and must be interpreted with considerable caution. Nevertheless, an admittedly crude estimate of the net program impact on the fertility of Mauritius can be obtained with the reasoning and procedure described below.

The earliest year for which birth data by age of mother in a continuous time series are available is 1955. An inspection of age-specific marital fertility rates for the 1955–1965 preprogram period shows that, except for women aged 30–34 and 45–49, fertility reached two peaks, one in 1956 or 1957 and one in 1963. Furthermore, the second peak exceeded the first in every case. Although fertility fell substantially during the last two preprogram years, the pattern of peaks precludes the derivation of simple projections based on 1955–1965 that imply post-implementation decline. Instead, simple projections for all but one age group would imply that most or all of the post–1965 marital fertility decline was a net program effect. This is unfortunate because, as just observed, continued modernization and rising abortion suggest that fertility decline would have continued after 1965 without the program. Given this situation, two types of projection assumptions are employed.

First, for women aged 30–34, whose second marital fertility peak was less than the first, a simple linear projection is calculated with means of the 1955–1960 and 1960–1965 rates. This method allows all the available information to be used, as well as providing a stable estimate of preprogram change that minimizes the effects of error for individual years. Second, for each remaining five-year age group the 1955–1959 period when data are reported by year of registration is

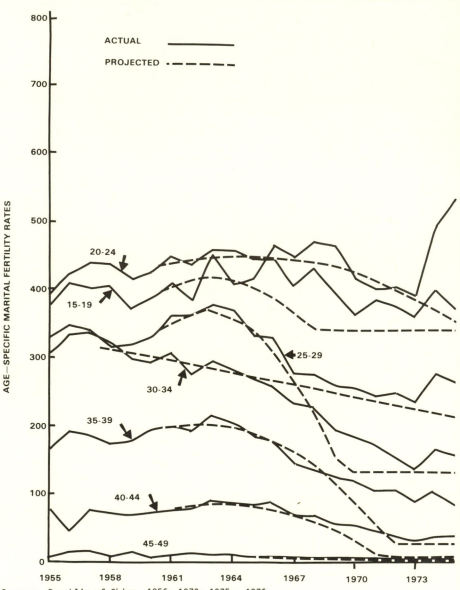

Source: Republic of China, 1956; 1973; 1975a; 1976.

Figure 11. Actual and Projected Age-Specific Marital Fertility Rates for Mauritius, 1955–1975

ignored and the data by year of occurrence for 1960–1965 are analyzed instead. Because the 1963 peak in these data occurs during the second half of the period, and also because the 1964 and 1965 rates are generally greater than the 1960–1962 rates, linear projections for

the 1960–1965 period would usually imply post-implementation increases. Consequently, the projection method adopted is to fit quadratic equations to the means of the fertility rates for each three succeeding two-year periods: 1960 and 1961, 1962 and 1963, and 1964
and 1965. These assumptions imply accelerating fertility decline. The
same procedures are used for women aged 45–49 since the linear assumption implies a net program effect of 105 percent.

The fertility rates from which the resulting projections are derived
are presented in Figure 11, and the resulting projections and the actual rates to which they are compared are also presented in Figure
11. As with projections for other countries, the age-specific marital
fertility rates for the United States are considered the lower limit of

**Table 15**
**Age-Specific Marital Fertility Rate Change and Crude Birth Rate**
**Decline in Mauritius Attributable to Net Program Effect Expressed**
**as Percentages by Age for 1965 to 1975**

| Net program effect on | Age | | | | | | |
|---|---|---|---|---|---|---|---|
| | 15-19 | 20-24 | 25-29 | 30-34 | 35-39 | 40-44 | 45-49 |
| Age-specific marital rate | 0 | 43 | 0 | 66 | 3 | 0 | 0 |
| Crude birth rate | 0 | 6 | 0 | 14 | 1 | 0 | 0 |

Source:   Mauritius, 1953; 1962; 1972; United Nations, 1966; 1970; 1976a.

possible decline. The overall results obtained from these procedures
indicate that about 21 percent of the total CBR reduction is a net program effect (Table 15).

More specifically, the results show that 66 percent of the age-specific marital fertility decline among women aged 30–34 is a net program effect. This implies that 14 percent of the CBR reduction is attributable to the net program hypothesis. Of course, this estimate
assumes that fertility decline without the program would have been
linear, but such decline might have accelerated, as discussed above.
If this is the case, the program's role is exaggerated. In sharp contrast, however, the estimates for five of the six remaining age groups,
which are derived assuming accelerating fertility decline, show negligible program effects. Only for women aged 20–24 is the program
effect substantial at 43 percent of the marital fertility decline. All together the program effect for these six age groups accounts for about
7 percent of the CBR reduction.

Unfortunately, the accuracy of the negligible effects found for women aged 15–19, 25–29, 35–39, and 40–44 is questionable because the marital fertility rates projected for these women are substantially less than the actual rates by the end of the period studied (Figure 11). This fact is prima facie evidence that the particular assumptions of accelerating decline that are employed in the projections are not sound. On the other hand, as noted above, the estimated program effect for women aged 30–34 would be too large if their fertility decline might have accelerated at least somewhat without the program. Taking into account these considerations, although it is possible that the net program effect is slightly less than the 21 percent of the CBR decline indicated in Table 15, it is probably best to interpret this estimate as the lower limit of the likely range within which the actual program effect almost certainly lies.

Moreover, a more realistic estimate of the lower limit of the probable program effect on the CBR can be derived by assuming that the best available estimate of the net program effect for a particular age group that is based on the assumption of accelerating fertility decline applies to all the other age groups. That is, assume the program effect of 43 percent for women aged 20–24 applies to all age groups, except women aged 15–19 who experienced an increase in marital fertility. This assumption produces the estimate that 34 percent of the CBR decline is a net program effect.

As noted above, it is possible that the program produced all of the marital fertility decline, and hence between 75 percent and 80 percent of the CBR reduction (ignoring women aged 15–19). This seems unlikely, however, since social and economic change continued unabated and abortions apparently increased after the program was implemented. A more realistic estimate of the upper limit of the range of the likely program effect can be obtained by assuming that the program effect for each age group is identical to the effect that was derived above for women aged 30–34 under the assumption of linear change. The estimated 66 percent of the marital fertility decline of women aged 30–34 is thus assumed to apply to all age groups. Ignoring women aged 15–19 this assumption produces an estimated upper limit for the net program effect of 51 percent of the CBR reduction.

## CONCLUSIONS

This analysis and the corresponding calculations suggest that between 34 percent and 51 percent of the CBR decline of Mauritius between 1965 and 1975 was a net program effect and that between 49 percent and 66 percent of the CBR decline was due to indigenous causes. Compared to the results obtained for Taiwan, South Korea, and Costa Rica, however, these results are probably subject to much greater error.

## VALIDITY OF THE FOUR CASE STUDIES

Because, as discussed in Chapter 3, self-selection, statistical regression, and experimental mortality do not bias the research design employed here in studying Taiwan, South Korea, Costa Rica, and Mauritius, the actual case studies are similarly unbiased. Instrumentation would, however, bias results if the data used in a particular case study were inadequate. Fortunately, the data used for Taiwan, Costa Rica, and Mauritius are of good to excellent quality. Although the birth data for South Korea are somewhat unreliable, two sets of fertility estimates have been developed by Cho (1973b) and Moon et al. (1973). Both data sets are employed in this research, and the close correspondence of the results based on each suggests that errors due to data unreliability are small. Therefore, the true values probably lie in the narrow range between the two estimates. Much of the noncensus year data for these countries were estimated by linear interpolation and extrapolation from census data. Since results based on alternative population estimates derived assuming geometric change are similar to the results based on linear population estimates, the linear assumptions appear to have introduced little error (see Appendix).

History and maturation are, potentially, more serious threats to the validity of these studies. These biases are mitigated, however, to the extent that historical and maturational forces act through change in the age-sex and marital status compositions, because the impact of change in these compositions is explicitly measured with the decomposition analysis. These threats are further minimized through the analysis of composition-specific fertility rates insofar as three criteria are met: (1) an extended preprogram period is studied, (2) maturational and historical forces are producing similar fertility change before and after program implementation, and (3) the character of the preprogram fertility change is accurately reflected in the projection assumptions.

With regard to the first criterion, the length of the preprogram period analyzed, the studies of Taiwan and Costa Rica are most adequate with periods encompassing nine and eleven years, followed by the study of Mauritius which encompasses periods of six to eleven years for different age groups, followed by the study of South Korea with a preprogram period of four years. The relative adequacy of the South Korean analysis is enhanced, however, by the use of simpler, more conservative assumptions of linear rather than accelerating fertility change.

On the second criterion, concerning the similarity of preprogram and post-implementation fertility change, maturation should produce little bias since virtually by definition it produces steady fertility change. Historical changes, on the other hand, are more likely to occur in discontinuous jumps and to produce corresponding discontinuities in fertility trends. As a variety of socioeconomic indicators show for the countries studied, however, socioeconomic development—the most important historical determinant of fertility change—continued without interruption and, according to many indicators, actually accelerated during the post-implementation period. Consequently, it is likely that historical changes in socioeconomic conditions would have continued to produce accelerating fertility decline in Taiwan, Costa Rica, and probably in South Korea and Mauritius, even in the absence of the family planning programs.

Turning to the third criterion, concerning how accurately the projection assumptions reflect the preprogram fertility change, general expectations and specific empirical evidence were brought to bear. First generally, various demographers have observed that even without family planning programs accelerating fertility change is to be expected in developing countries. More specifically, empirical inspections of preprogram fertility changes found for most age groups that they often implied accelerating fertility declines in three of the countries, and equally important, as noted above, various statistical indicators suggest that socioeconomic change was accelerating in these countries during the periods encompassed by the present research. Projection assumptions were based on this empirical evidence insofar as permitted by the quality of available demographic data.

Instability in preprogram fertility trends is the final potential source of bias, and the one that appears to have been most important in determining the actual relative validity of the results of the case studies conducted here. This bias was thoroughly assessed in the discussion of results for specific countries. On this criterion, the results for Taiwan and South Korea are best because they rest upon the analysis of relatively large populations. The results for the relatively small Costa Rican population are less adequate, but the procedures employed to study Costa Rica allow the magnitude of the net program effect to be estimated within a fairly narrow range. Regrettably, because of the obvious, substantial instability in the marital fertility rates for the tiny population of Mauritius, the results are subject to considerable bias. In order to minimize the impact of these biases, a range of probable program effect estimates was derived. Although the width of the range reflects some of the uncertainty due to instability in the trends for Mauritius, the relatively lengthy chain of reasoning upon which it is based suggests that the results should be interpreted with considerable caution.

Overall, the interrupted time series design developed here is less biased than much previous research dealing with the impact of family planning programs on fertility in third world countries. As a result the conclusions are more strongly supported. More specifically, the results for the case studies of Taiwan and South Korea are the most valid. They indicate that approximately 11 percent of the 1964–1975 CBR decline in Taiwan and between 1 percent and 10 percent of the 1965–1971 decline in South Korea are net program effects, while the remaining 89 percent and 90 percent to 99 percent are due to ongoing social and economic development or other indigenous causes. Somewhat less valid are the results for Costa Rica which suggest that between 4 percent and 23 percent but probably closer to 4 percent of the 1967–1971 decline is due to the program, while the remaining 77 percent to 96 percent but probably closer to 96 percent is due to indigenous secular change. The least valid results, those for Mauritius, imply that between 34 percent and 51 percent of the CBR decline may be a net progam effect. Although these results provide some support for the position that advocates the independent efficacy of family planning programs, it must be noted that in three of the four cases the programs play a relatively small role.

In terms of points shaved off the CBR, the largest but least valid estimate of a net program effect is the one for Mauritius, three to six points in ten years. More reliable are the estimates for Taiwan, South Korea, and Costa Rica which range from 0.1 to 1.6 points during periods of four to eleven years. Nevertheless, the evidence suggests that the CBR declines in these countries were dominated by continuing change in social, economic, demographic, and additional indigenous conditions.

## NOTES

1. The desire to avoid manual labor among the more educated, and the increasing competition for high status occupations is described in greater detail by Benedict (1958: 318–321, 328), Titmuss and Abel-Smith (1968: 12, 72, 103–104), Meade et al. (1968: 60–61, 204), and Wright (1974: 45).

2. Xenos (1970: 3) reports that assuming constant boundaries, the percentage of the population living in urban areas rose slightly from 31 percent to 34 percent between 1952 and 1962. Allowing changes in the boundaries as of 1962 produces the much larger estimate of 44 percent. When places as small as 5,000 inhabitants are considered urban, a substantial jump in percent urban from 30 to 42 is found between 1950 and 1960 (Davis, 1969: 61).

# 8

# Cross-National Approaches to Estimating Total Socioeconomic and Independent Program Effects for the Third World

As reflected in the critical analysis of Chapter 2 and in other reviews of the literature (Chandrasekaran and Hermalin, 1975; Forrest and Ross, 1978; Ross and Forrest, 1978; United Nations, 1978; 1979b; Hernandez, 1981a), most studies of family planning programs focus on a single country. In the most recent and most ambitious of the few cross-national studies, however, national-level data for nearly 90 countries are used to estimate the extent to which variations in fertility declines in the third world are an independent effect of organized family planning programs (Mauldin and Berelson, 1978a; Tsui and Bogue, 1978).

A lively debate followed in the wake of these two studies with Demeny (1979a; 1979b) and Dixon (1978b) seriously questioning the adequacy of the theoretical justification and the methodological underpinnings for calculations used to obtain empirical estimates (see also Mauldin and Berelson, 1978b; Bogue and Tsui, 1979a; 1979b; Hernandez, 1981b). Growing out of central arguments in this debate and additional theoretical and methodological inquiries, this chapter develops an assessment of analytical strategies that provides a more firmly grounded basis for deriving estimates of the independent impact that family planning programs had on variation in fertility change in much of the third world during the late 1960s and early 1970s.

## THEORETICAL MODEL

The macro-level theory addressed in this section, which is schematically represented in Figure 12, focuses on national socioeconomic structures and processes, aggregate demographic change, and family planning programs as instruments of national and international policy. At this macro level, the socioeconomic setting refers to a broad

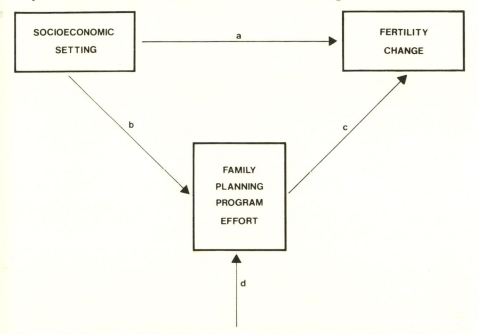

Figure 12. Theoretical Model for Analyzing the Independent Effect of Family Planning Programs on Fertility Change in the Third World

array of social, economic, institutional, and cultural factors that can influence fertility either directly or indirectly.

The socioeconomic setting is viewed as influencing aggregate fertility *directly* by generating the demand for and use of nonprogram means of limiting births, as discussed in Chapter 1. Hence cross-national variation in national socioeconomic settings can influence cross-national variation in fertility change. This *direct socioeconomic effect* is represented by path "a" in Figure 12.

The socioeconomic setting also can influence aggregate fertility *indirectly* by generating the demand for and use of program supplied means of limiting births, as discussed in Chapter 1, but also because

it represents the infrastructure and the sociopolitical context that influence the extent to which family planning programs can and will be
implemented by political leaders. For example, the socioeconomic setting encompasses the transportation, communications, and adminis-
trative/bureaucratic infrastructures that influence the magnitude of
the program effort that can be mounted in a particular country (Godwin, 1975: 78; Demerath, 1976: 84). In addition, because the socioeconomic setting encompasses the sociopolitical context, it influences the
extent to which political leaders are able and willing to pursue family
planning programs. For example, family planning policies may be implemented by political leaders in reaction to an obvious demand for
birth control methods that is reflected in a prior decline in aggregate
fertility (Godwin, 1975: 82; Demeny, 1979a: 151). Alternatively, faced
with multiple demands on extremely scarce resources, political leaders especially in poor third world countries may react by not adopting
a family planning policy or, if they adopt one, by pursuing the program with only limited vigor (Godwin, 1975: 84–85). Through these
mechanisms, cross-national variation in national socioeconomic settings can indirectly influence cross-national variation in fertility change
by influencing cross-national variation in levels of family planning
program effort. The *indirect socioeconomic effects* are represented by
the conjunction of paths "b" and "c" in Figure 12.

In short, macro-level socioeconomic structures and processes can
influence aggregate fertility directly by generating the demand for and
use of nonprogram means of limiting births, but they also can influence aggregate fertility trends indirectly, because they represent the
indigenous demand for program supplied birth control methods as well
as the infrastructure and the political context that influence the extent to which family planning programs can and will be implemented
by government leaders.

Taking family planning programs as the point of reference, the *indirect socioeconomic effect* can be referred to as the *mediating effect of
family planning programs* since the programs are mediating between
aggregate fertility change and the causally prior influence on program effort of the infrastructural and sociopolitical context inherent
in the socioeconomic setting. This *mediating effect* also can be referred to as the *facilitating effect of family planning programs* since
program supplied birth control is facilitating the fertility change that
is driven by socioeconomic and other indigenous forces.

Alternatively, macro-level *independent program effects* also are theoretically possible. For example, if political leaders in third world
countries perceive a long-term value to family planning programs that
transcends immediate socioeconomic needs or concerns, they might take
a proactive stance in pursuing family planning policies. Or these political leaders might pursue a family planning policy, regardless of the

internal socioeconomic setting, because of information, encouragement, or pressure from extra-national agencies, such as foreign donors or governments of more developed countries who also provide aid,
investment, or trade opportunities (Godwin, 1975: 83–84; Sinding and
Hemmer, 1975: 276). In short, the family planning impact on aggregate fertility is independent of the socioeconomic setting to the extent
that it results from political decisions in third world countries that, in
the senses described above, either are proactive or are responses to
extra-national factors, such as the efforts of international donor agencies. These possibilities are represented by the conjunction of paths
"d" and "c" in Figure 12.

    In deriving empirical estimates based on the macro-level theoreti-
cal model developed here, the present monograph employs procedures
that provide means to distinguish between: (1) the total effect (combined direct and indirect effects) of the socioeconomic setting on fertility, and (2) the independent effect of family planning programs on
fertility.[1] Since nations are the unit of analysis in this study, conclusions drawn refer only to theoretical notions that pertain directly to
this aggregate level.[2]

    Hence, in the remainder of the present study the socioeconomic ef-
fect refers to cross-national variation in aggregate fertility change that
is accounted for by cross-national variation in the socioeconomic setting, interpreted theoretically as representing cross-national variation in the socioeconomic determinants of fertility and the socioeconomic, infrastructural, and sociopolitical determinants of family
planning program effort. Similarly, the independent family planning
program effect refers to cross-national variation in aggregate fertility
change that is accounted for by cross-national variation in family
planning program effort that results from the proactive initiatives of
government leaders and responses by government leaders to extra-
national agencies, insofar as these are independent of cross-national
variation in socioeconomic settings.

## METHODOLOGICAL PROBLEMS AND APPROACHES

    In criticizing recent cross-national studies, Demeny (1979a; 1979b)
calls attention to a fundamental problem confronting any effort, as
discussed here in Chapter 2, to accurately estimate the independent
program effect on fertility, namely the difficulty in empirically disentangling any genuinely independent program effect from the causally
prior effect of the numerous socioeconomic determinants of fertility
change. Demeny (1979a: 149) emphasizes that "program effort (as
measured in an observed historical sample) may be a reflection of underlying fertility determinants not grasped by the available socioeconomic indicators."

Demeny is effectively pointing up the theoretical need for multiple indicators that measure, as fully as possible, every relevant aspect of the socioeconomic setting. Although it is not possible to measure all relevant features of the socioeconomic milieu, and hence, to insure perfect content validity (Carmines and Zeller, 1979), the larger and more comprehensive the set of indicators included in a particular empirical analysis, the smaller will be the bias that exaggerates the independent impact of the programs (see also Hernandez, 1981a; 1981b). Therefore, the cross-national analyses developed in the next chapter reduce the magnitude of this bias, compared to past studies, by increasing the number and breadth of socioeconomic indicators that are included.[3]

Dixon (1978b), however, points up a major difficulty associated with using multiple measures of the socioeconomic setting in the present theoretical and empirical context. Empirically, the difficulty is in distinguishing between the effects of theoretically distinct components of the socioeconomic setting, particularly when, as is necessarily the case in a cross-national study encompassing a large number of third world countries, the choice of which components to include and which to exclude from consideration is somewhat arbitrarily based on the availability or lack of availability of relevant data. Methodologically, the difficulty is that the use of multiple regression analysis to distinguish the effects of theoretically distinct socioeconomic components is undermined by multicollinearity among the socioeconomic indicators which leads to unstable regression coefficients.

The potential empirical difficulty associated with deriving separate estimates for various socioeconomic components is avoided in the present study by focusing empirically and theoretically only on the total socioeconomic effect and the independent program effect. It should be emphasized, however, that the socioeconomic indicators should be interpreted as precisely that—*indicators* reflecting interrelated aspects of the socioeconomic setting.

The corresponding methodological difficulty of multicollinearity among the socioeconomic indicators, namely instability in the regression coefficients, is avoided in the present study by deriving estimates based on multiple correlation coefficients. Although methodological inquiries often recommend the use of multiple regression coefficients or analogous parameters (Duncan, 1975; Alwin and Hauser, 1975; Fox, 1980; Stolzenberg, 1979), multiple correlation coefficients are preferable in the present study, because a cluster of indicators is required to adequately measure the full domain of substantive content of a complex variable, namely the socioeconomic setting (Namboodiri, Carter, and Blalock, 1975: 189–190; Carmines and Zeller, 1979).

Furthermore, although the possibility has not been raised explicitly in past inquiries, multicollinearity might appear to undermine the stability and the substantive interpretability of the estimates of the total socioeconomic effect and the independent program effect, because of the relatively large zero-order correlations between the socioeconomic indicators and the program effort index. In the present theoretical context, however, such an obstacle to interpretability is not present (Gordon, 1968), because clear conceptual distinctions have been drawn between the socioeconomic setting and family planning program activities, and because a clear causal order can be presumed to link these two variables, namely the socioeconomic setting influences program effort without feedback for the period studied.

Following from these considerations, and to insure that the net program effect estimate is in fact independent of the causally prior socioeconomic effects on program effort and fertility, each of the analytical strategies employed in the present research allocates to the estimate of the total socioeconomic effect the entire joint influence that the socioeconomic setting and the program have on fertility. Only then is the remaining influence of the program on fertility allocated to the independent program effect. No effort is made to empirically distinguish the direct and the indirect effects of the socioeconomic setting.

## METHODOLOGICAL OPPORTUNITIES

Two important methodological opportunities are inherent in the analysis of the present cross-national study. First, the two most recent cross-national studies employ sets of socioeconomic indicators which are related conceptually, but which are not identical. Hence, by conducting parallel analyses with the two sets of indicators their relative adequacy can be compared. Second, these two studies employ different dependent variables, namely the crude birth rate and the total fertility rate. Entwisle (1981) recently used one analytical approach with data for each type of rate to provide evidence on differences in conclusions that result from using one or the other fertility measure. The present research provides another opportunity, but with a different approach, to offer such evidence through parallel analyses using these two fertility measures.

To take best advantage of these opportunities, a single set of countries should be used in all of the empirical analyses. An inspection of the data from the two recent studies shows that a combined data set can be created for a total of 83 countries. Hence, the analyses and conclusions of the present study pertain to these 83 countries.

The other major difference between the two recent studies is that they employ a variety of analytical strategies to develop program effect estimates. This raises the following question. Which of the several plausible analytical strategies is the most appropriate one for deriving estimates of the total socioeconomic effect and the independent program effect on fertility change? The next section addresses this question by evaluating the biases associated with five distinct variations of the posttest-only and nonequivalent control group designs. Given existing data, these five analytical strategies are the best that can be used to study the cross-national success of family planning programs.

## FIVE ANALYTICAL STRATEGIES

The first analytical strategy discussed here consists of two stages. First, fertility at time 2 is regressed on the socioeconomic indicators for an earlier time, and the coefficient of determination ($R_1^2$), corrected for the number of socioeconomic indicators included as independent variables, is calculated.[4] The result estimates the proportion of the variation in fertility that is accounted for by the socioeconomic indicators. Second, fertility at time 2 is regressed both on the same socioeconomic indicators and on the index of family planning program effort. Then the coefficient of determination is calculated ($R_2^2$). The increment, beyond the socioeconomic effect, in the variation in fertility that is accounted for by the program is calculated by subtracting the coefficient of determination obtained in the first stage from the coefficient of determination obtained from this second stage ($R_2^2 - R_1^2$).[5]

This strategy tends to overestimate the impact of the socioeconomic setting on *fertility change*, because it fails to take separate account of the fertility level at the beginning of the time period under study (see Bohrnstedt [1969] for a discussion abstracted from any specific substantive context). In other words, this procedure analyzes the entire variation in fertility at time 2 as if it represented nothing other than fertility change. But it actually includes not only the *fertility change between time 1 and time 2*, but also *variation in fertility at time 1*. Since the variation in fertility at time 1 should be excluded from an assessment of the total socioeconomic effect on *fertility change*, the actual magnitude of the socioeconomic effect is overestimated using this analytical strategy.

As a result, the independent program effect is probably underestimated, as reflected in the following reasoning. Recall that the entire program effect can be partitioned conceptually into two distinct components: the independent effect and the mediating effect. Now, since the mediating effect is due to the socioeconomic setting, and since the total socioeconomic effect is overestimated with this analytical strategy, it is likely that the indirect component of the total socioeconomic effect also is overestimated. Insofar as the indirect socioeconomic effect is overestimated, the mediating portion of the program effect also is overestimated. But if the mediating effect of the program is overestimated, the independent program effect on fertility change is underestimated by a corresponding magnitude.

The second analytical strategy consists of the same two stages as the first, except that a measure of fertility at time 1 is included as an independent variable in the calculation of both coefficients of determination ($R_3^2$ and $R_4^2$). This strategy takes account of fertility at time 1, but in the interpretation of the coefficient of determination derived in the first stage ($R_3^2$), all of the covariation between fertility at time 2 and fertility at time 1 is attributed to the socioeconomic setting. Since this covariation should not be attributed to socioeconomic factors that influence fertility change *between time 1 and time 2*, this approach leads to an overestimate of the role of the socioeconomic setting. It then follows from the reasoning developed above in conjunction with the first analytical strategy that the mediating effect of family planning programs is probably overestimated and the independent impact (calculated as $R_4^2 - R_3^2$) is probably underestimated.

A third analytical strategy that might appear to overcome these difficulties, one which was employed by Mauldin and Berelson (1978a), is the same as the first analytical strategy discussed above, except that the absolute change in fertility between time 1 and time 2 replaces fertility at time 2 as the dependent variable in the calculation of both coefficients of determination ($R_5^2$ and $R_6^2$). As reflected in the discussion of Cohen and Cohen (1975: 381–382), however, the results are biased unless a bivariate correlation equal to zero is found to obtain between fertility at time 1 and fertility change between times 1 and 2.[6] In the empirical cases presented here, this correlation coefficient is negative, and hence the dependent variable (absolute change in fertility) "undercorrects" the fertility at time 2 for the fertility at time 1, as did the preceding analytical strategies, and the socioeconomic effect is overestimated. As discussed above in conjunction with the first analytical strategy, since the socioeconomic effect ($R_5^2$) is overestimated, the independent program effect ($R_6^2 - R_5^2$) is probably underestimated.

The fourth analytical strategy, one also used by Mauldin and Berelson (1978a), is similar to the third except that percentage change in fertility replaces absolute change as the dependent variable. But percentage change is also a "gain" score, and in the present empirical context it too is negatively correlated with fertility at time 1. Hence, the percentage change score also "undercorrects" the fertility at time

2, and the result is the overestimation of the socioeconomic effect ($R_7^2$), and the probable underestimation of the independent program effect ($R_8^2 - R_7^2$).

The fifth, and final, analytical strategy consists of three stages described by Tsui and Bogue (1978; Bogue and Tsui, 1979b). First, fertility at time 2 is regressed on fertility at time 1. The coefficient of determination ($r_1^2$) is calculated to estimate the proportion of the variation in fertility at time 2 that is due to variation in fertility at time 1. This result is subtracted from 1.0, that is, the total variation in fertility at time 2, in order to estimate the variation in fertility at time 2 that is *not* accounted for by variation in fertility at time 1 ($1.0 - r_1^2$). In other words, this estimates the proportion of the variation in fertility at time 2 that is accounted for by fertility change between time 1 and time 2.

The second stage in Tsui and Bogue's analytical strategy regresses fertility at time 2 on fertility at time 1 and on the socioeconomic indicators (same as $R_3^2$ above). The value of the coefficient of determination from the first stage ($r_1^2$) is subtracted from the value of the coefficient of determination obtained in the second stage ($R_3^2$) to estimate the proportion of the variation in fertility at time 2 that is due to socioeconomic factors ($R_3^2 - r_1^2$) independently of fertility at time 1. This result is then divided by the (previously calculated) estimate of the proportion of the variation in fertility at time 2 that is accounted for by fertility change ($1.0 - r_1^2$) in order to estimate the proportion of the fertility change that is due to socioeconomic factors independently of fertility at time 1. The second stage calculations can be summarized as follows:[7]

$$\frac{(R_3^2 - r_1^2)}{(1.0 - r_1^2)}$$

If it is assumed that socioeconomic factors influence fertility change, but that a time lag is needed for the fertility change to occur, and if it can be assumed that fertility at an earlier date does not influence the socioeconomic factors which then influence fertility, it follows that the fifth analytical strategy provides an unbiased estimate of the extent to which fertility change is accounted for by socioeconomic factors (for abstract discussions see Bohrnstedt, 1969; Cohen and Cohen, 1975).

Finally, as the third stage of Tsui and Bogue's analytical strategy, fertility at time 2 is regressed on fertility at time 1, on the socioeconomic indicators, and on the index of family planning program effort. The coefficient of determination from the second stage ($R_3^2$) is then subtracted from the coefficient from this third stage (same as $R_4^2$ above) in order to estimate the proportion of the variation in fertility at time

2 that is an independent program effect ($R_4^2 - R_3^2$). The result is divided by the previously calculated estimate of the proportion of fertility at time 2 that is accounted for by fertility change ($1.0 - r_1^2$) in order to estimate the proportion of the fertility change that is an independent program effect. The calculations from stage three are summarized as follows:

$$\frac{(R_4^2 - R_3^2)}{(1.0 - r_1^2)}$$

This is an unbiased estimate, given the assumptions cited earlier. The implications of assumptions which are different, but plausible in the present empirical context, are discussed below in Chapter 9 following the derivation of estimates of the total socioeconomic and independent program effects.

## NOTES

1. The terms "total effect" and "independent effect" are used here in the sense exemplified in cases 3 and 3(b) of Duncan's (1970: 42) discussion.

2. Any theoretical interpretation of the data analyzed here that referred to micro-level effects within nations would suffer from the ecological fallacy (Robinson, 1950; Alker, 1969; United Nations, 1979b: 98).

3. This general approach was employed earlier by Hernandez (1981b), but the present effort goes far beyond the earlier one, which simply adopted the specific analytical strategy of Mauldin and Berelson (1978a). The current effort systematically evaluates the relative adequacy, and then implements five different analytical strategies that are plausible candidates, prima facie, for estimating the total socioeconomic and the independent program effects.

4. See Cohen and Cohen (1975), Johnson (1972), and Loether and McTavish (1976) for discussions of the correction or adjustment procedure. All the results in this monograph are adjusted for the number of independent variables by using this procedure.

5. As noted above, calculating procedures using $R^2$s that are described in this section are based on the cluster of indicators approach recommended by Namboodiri, Carter, and Blalock (1975). These procedures are analogous to the one described by Duncan (1970: 42).

6. Bohrnstedt (1969: 118) mentions this in the context of deriving the appropriate analytical strategy. Cohen and Cohen (1975: 381–382) also discuss this in terms of regression coefficients.

7. In other terminology, this is a means of calculating the relevant multiple-partial correlation coefficient (Namboodiri, Carter, and Blalock, 1975: 189) between fertility at time 2 and the cluster of socioeconomic indicators, controlling for fertility at time 1.

# 9

## Alternative Estimates of the Total Socioeconomic and Independent Program Effects for the Third World

### THE TOTAL SOCIOECONOMIC EFFECT

Mauldin and Berelson (1978a) compiled CBR data for 1965 and 1975, socioeconomic indicators for 1970, and an index of family planning program effort circa 1972. Tsui and Bogue (1978) presented estimates of the total fertility rate (TFR) for 1968 and 1975, and socioeconomic indicators circa 1968, using the family planning data presented by Mauldin and Berelson (1978a).[1]

Based on these data, new alternative estimates of the total socioeconomic effect on fertility change are presented in Table 16. The panels on the left half of the table present results using the CBR as the dependent variable, and the panels on the right present results using the TFR as the dependent variable. The upper panels use as independent variables the seven socioeconomic indicators (1–7) employed by Mauldin and Berelson (1978a), supplemented with indicators for three additional factors (8–10) which they found to be important in "qualitative" analyses. The lower panels use as independent variables the five socioeconomic indicators (11–15) employed by Tsui and Bogue (1978), supplemented with another indicator (16) for which they compiled data, and one indicator (7) from Mauldin and Berelson (1978a). These seven indicators in the lower panels are selected to produce a set that conceptually corresponds closely to the seven indicators employed by Mauldin and Berelson. Then the three additional "qualitative" indicators (8–10) from the upper panels are also included.

**Table 16**
**The Total Impact of the Socioeconomic Setting on Fertility Change in the Third World during the Late 1960s and Early 1970s**[a]

| Socioeconomic Indicators[b] | Analytical Strategies Implemented with Crude Birth Rate | | | | | Analytical Strategies Implemented with Total Fertility Rate | | | | |
|---|---|---|---|---|---|---|---|---|---|---|
| | 1 | 2 | 3 | 4 | 5 | 1 | 2 | 3 | 4 | 5 |
| Initial Indicators from Mauldin and Berelson | | | | | | | | | | |
| 1-7 | 68 | 90 | 55 | 59 | 23 | 50 | 80 | 25 | 35 | 26 |
| 1-10 | 80 | 92 | 66 | 74 | 38 | 65 | 81 | 26 | 41 | 32 |
| Initial Indicators from Tsui and Bogue | | | | | | | | | | |
| 11-15 | 63 | 90 | 48 | 52 | 16 | 49 | 77 | 19 | 26 | 17 |
| 11-16, 7 | 71 | 91 | 55 | 59 | 23 | 54 | 79 | 23 | 33 | 24 |
| 11-16, 7-10 | 79 | 92 | 65 | 72 | 37 | 64 | 80 | 25 | 38 | 28 |

a--The percentage of the variation in fertility change for 83 third world countries.
b--Socioeconomic indicators from the quantitative analysis of Mauldin and Berelson (1978a).

  1.  GNP per capita
  2.  Infant mortality
  3.  Percent of population in cities 100,000+
  4.  Percent of males aged 15-64 in nonagricultural labor force
  5.  Primary and secondary school enrollment
  6.  Life expectancy
  7.  Adults literate

Additional socioeconomic indicators from Mauldin and Berelson (1978a) that are incorporated in the present analysis

  8.  Island-status
  9.  Pace of social change
  10. 1970 population density

Socioeconomic indicators included in the quantitative analysis of Tsui and Bogue (1978), plus a sixth for which they compiled data.

  11. GNP per capita
  12. Infant mortality
  13. Percent urban
  14. Percent of employed females in agriculture
  15. Female school enrollment ratio.
  16. Life expectancy

Starting with the upper left quadrant of Table 16, the difference between the values in the first and second rows reflects the increase in the estimated magnitude of the total socioeconomic effect that is obtained by including the cluster of three "qualitative" socioeconomic indicators along with the cluster of seven employed by Mauldin and Berelson (1978a).[2] As suggested by earlier discussions of the value of incorporating additional socioeconomic indicators into any particular analysis, the addition of the cluster of three indicators to the original cluster of seven in each analytical strategy does, in fact, lead to an increase in the estimated magnitude of the total socioeconomic effect. Only with analytical strategy #2, which attributes all the covariation between fertility at times 1 and 2 to socioeconomic factors, is the increase in the socioeconomic effect as small as 2 percent. In other cases the increase ranges from 11 percent to 15 percent.

The evaluation in the previous chapter of these analytical strategies is supported by the pattern of results. This evaluation suggested that, compared to strategy #5, the other strategies would tend to over-estimate the socioeconomic effect. The results obtained from various strategies show differences of considerable magnitude in the expected direction.

The first row in the lower left quadrant in Table 16 presents results similar to those in the first row of the upper left quadrant, except that they are based on the five socioeconomic indicators employed by Tsui and Bogue (1978: 31) in their multivariate analysis. These indicators reflect socioeconomic dimensions that are fairly closely related, conceptually, to dimensions reflected in five of the indicators employed by Mauldin and Berelson (1978a). Both studies use per capita GNP and infant mortality, and both use indicators reflecting urbanization, the mix of employment in the agricultural and nonagricultural sectors, and school enrollments (see Table 16).

By incorporating another socioeconomic indicator (life expectancy) for which Tsui and Bogue compiled data, and one additional socio-economic indicator from Mauldin and Berelson (adults literate[3]) into the analysis using the five socioeconomic indicators employed by Tsui and Bogue, estimates that are fairly comparable, conceptually, to those based on the Mauldin and Berelson indicators can be derived. The results of this analysis, which are presented in the second row of the lower left quadrant in Table 16, are quite similar, empirically, to the ones in the top row of the upper left quadrant.

The next row in the lower left quadrant presents results obtained by incorporating the cluster of three "qualitative" variables into the analysis. Again, the magnitudes of the estimates in this series are quite similar to the corresponding estimates based solely on data from Mauldin and Berelson. Four of the five new estimates are slightly smaller than the corresponding estimates in the upper left quadrant, however, suggesting that the indicators employed by Mauldin and Berelson may, overall, provide a slightly more adequate estimate of the socioeconomic effect, as judged in terms of the argument about the value of multiple indicators for measuring as fully as possible the socioeconomic effect.

The panels in the right half of Table 16 present results obtained in the same fashion as those on the left, except that the TFR replaces the CBR in each analysis. The general patterns of results on the left and right sides of the table are the same, although the magnitudes of the estimates are rather different. In the first four analytical strategies the estimates for the TFR are substantially less than the corresponding estimates for the CBR.

For the fifth analytical strategy the effects for the TFR are slightly larger in the estimates based on clusters of five or seven socioeconomic indicators, but notably smaller in the estimates based on the cluster of ten. A comparison of the upper and lower quadrants on the right side shows that the estimates based solely on indicators from Mauldin and Berelson again appear slightly more adequate than the estimates that depend partly on indicators from Tsui and Bogue.

Overall, the most adequate results obtained using the appropriate analytical strategy (#5) suggest that for the 83 countries studied socioeconomic factors account for about 38 percent of the variation in CBR change between 1965 and 1975, and 32 percent of the variation in TFR change between 1968 and 1975. The substantial difference between the two sets of estimates may be due, in part, to the different time periods analyzed and differences in data quality, but it seems likely that much of the difference is due to the fact that part of the CBR change is associated with change in the age-sex structure, and this may be associated for a variety of reasons with the socioeconomic indicators (see Entwisle, 1981), whereas change in the TFR is independent of the age-sex structure.

## THE INDEPENDENT EFFECT OF FAMILY PLANNING PROGRAMS

Estimates of the independent program effect, which are presented in Table 17, also support the methodological evaluation of the analytical strategies that was developed in Chapter 8. This evaluation suggested that, compared to strategy #5, the other strategies would probably underestimate the independent program effect. The results in Table 17 show that, in 39 of the 40 possible comparisons of specific sets of independent and dependent variables, the estimates from strategy #5 are larger than the estimates from other strategies. In addition, as was true of the socioeconomic results, in the estimates based on the clusters of ten socioeconomic indicators, the indicators drawn solely from Mauldin and Berelson (1978a) appear slightly more adequate than estimates depending partly on indicators from Tsui and Bogue (1978).

Additional conclusions to be drawn from Table 17 concern similarities and differences in the results for the CBR and TFR. The differences in corresponding estimates for analytical strategies #1 and #2 are quite small. For strategies #3 and #4 the differences are substantial when based on clusters of 5 or 7 indicators, but small when based on clusters of 10 indicators. Finally, differences for the most appropriate strategy (#5) are substantial in every case, with the program estimates for the TFR only about one-half the size of the corresponding CBR estimates. Although these differences may be due partly to

**Table 17**

**The Independent Impact of Family Planning Programs on Fertility Change in the Third World during the Late 1960s and Early 1970s[a]**

| Socioeconomic Indicators[b] | Analytical Strategies Implemented with Crude Birth Rate | | | | | Analytical Strategies Implemented with Total Fertility Rate | | | | |
|---|---|---|---|---|---|---|---|---|---|---|
| | 1 | 2 | 3 | 4 | 5 | 1 | 2 | 3 | 4 | 5 |
| Initial Indicators from Mauldin and Berelson | | | | | | | | | | |
| 1-7 | 10 | 4 | 22 | 20 | 35 | 10 | 4 | 9 | 10 | 13 |
| 1-10 | 3 | 3 | 12 | 8 | 22 | 2 | 3 | 11 | 8 | 10 |
| Initial Indicators from Tsui and Bogue | | | | | | | | | | |
| 11-15 | 17 | 5 | 29 | 28 | 42 | 16 | 6 | 14 | 17 | 20 |
| 11-16, 7 | 11 | 4 | 22 | 22 | 35 | 11 | 4 | 9 | 11 | 14 |
| 11-16, 7-10 | 4 | 4 | 13 | 9 | 24 | 3 | 4 | 12 | 9 | 13 |

a--The percentage of the variation in fertility change for 83 third world countries.
b--Socioeconomic indicators included in the quantitative Analysis of Mauldin and Berelson (1978a).

1. GNP per capita
2. Infant mortality
3. Percent of population in cities 100,000+
4. Percent of males aged 15-64 in nonagricultural labor force
5. Primary and secondary school enrollment
6. Life expectancy
7. Adults literate

Additional socioeconomic indicators from Mauldin and Berelson (1978a) that are incorporated in the present Analysis

8. Island-status
9. Pace of social change
10. 1970 population density

Socioeconomic indicators included in the quantitative analysis of Tsui and Bogue (1978), plus a sixth for which they compiled data.

11. GNP per capita
12. Infant mortality
13. Percent urban
14. Percent of employed females in agriculture
15. Female school enrollment ratio.
16. Life expectancy

variations in the quality of the fertility data and the time periods analyzed, the most important reason for these differences is probably that CBR change includes variation associated with shifts in the age-sex structure, while TFR change does not. The nature of this age-sex effect warrants detailed examination, because it provides an important justification in the present substantive context for preferring independent program effect estimates derived with the TFR to those based on the CBR.

Why is this the case? First, both theoretical and mathematical arguments imply that covariation between program effort and CBR change is, at least partly, a spurious consequence of cross-national differentials in the age-sex compositions of various populations. Theoretically, compared to countries with relatively small proportions who are women in the prime childbearing ages, countries with relatively large proportions of such women will, other things equal, tend to have a greater demand for birth control methods. Hence, these countries will be able to implement family planning programs more easily than countries with relatively few women in the prime childbearing ages, and there will be corresponding cross-national differentials in fertility.

Mathematically, among countries with identical declines in age-specific fertility rates, it is a mathematical necessity that countries with relatively fewer women in the prime childbearing ages will experience smaller CBR declines. In this situation, because countries with relatively more women in the prime childbearing ages will tend to have both a more vigorous family planning program and a more rapid CBR decline, if an empirical indicator of the age-sex composition is not explicitly included in the analysis, the CBR change which should be attributed to the causally prior differential in age-sex composition will instead be allocated, inappropriately, to the independent program effect.

In contrast, because TFR change is independent of age-sex composition differentials, in the present example there will be no differential TFR change to inappropriately allocate to the independent program effect. Consequently, if the TFR is used as the dependent variable, changes in fertility that actually are due to differentials in the age-sex composition will not be confounded with any independent program effect, as they will be if the CBR is employed as the dependent variable.

Beyond these spurious effects, any genuinely independent program effect will tend to influence the CBR in two countervailing directions. First, it will produce a relative decline in the number of births and, hence, in the numerator of the CBR and in the overall CBR. But, because an independent program effect reduces the relative size of the youngest cohorts, the cohorts who are too young to bear children, it also tends to reduce the size of the denominator of the CBR, which as a mathematical artifact tends to increase the overall CBR. In contrast, an independent program effect will tend to reduce the numerator of the TFR without affecting the denominator, producing only a relative decline in the TFR. Consequently, compared to estimates derived with the CBR, those based on the TFR will more faithfully measure the independent program effect on aggregate fertility *decline*.

Now, in the present empirical analyses the socioeconomic indicators may reduce, to some extent, the magnitude of the age-sex biases in the program effect estimates derived with the CBR, because these indicators can be related for various reasons to cross-national differentials in age-sex composition. On the other hand, it is unlikely that the socioeconomic indicators fully measure the age-sex effect. Hence, it is also unlikely that the estimates of the independent program effect based on the CBR suffer no age-sex bias. Consequently, because an adequate measure of age-sex composition is not available for the 83 third world countries studied here, the remainder of the chapter employs only the independent program effect estimates based on the TFR in perference to estimates derived with the CBR.

Taking into account all the theoretical, methodological, and empirical arguments which have been presented to this point regarding the quality of various cross-national estimates of the independent program effect, the best estimate is the one using research design #5 with the TFR and with the maximum number of socioeconomic indicators drawn solely from Mauldin and Berelson. This estimate suggests that, independently of socioeconomic factors, the programs account for about 10 percent of the variation in fertility change during the late 1960s and early 1970s for the 83 third world countries studied here.

## BIASES IN THE BEST ESTIMATES

For two major reasons, however, the 10 percent estimate should be considered the upper limit of the probable range of the independent effect of family planning programs at the macro-level. First, as discussed by Demeny (1979a; 1979b) and in Chapter 2, since not all relevant features of the socioeconomic context can be measured and included in any particular empirical estimate, any estimate will tend to overestimate the independent program effect. Most notably, the present estimates do not include an indicator reflecting the marital status composition of women, a factor which might account for an important portion of fertility change.

This marital composition effect, which is analogous to the age-sex composition effect discussed above, is founded upon both theoretical and mathematical arguments implying that covariation between program effort and TFR change is, at least partly, a spurious consequence of cross-national differentials in marital status composition. Theoretically, compared to countries in which relatively large proportions of women in the childbearing ages are married, countries with smaller proportions married will tend, other things equal, to experience a smaller demand for birth control methods. Hence, these countries will experience greater difficulty in implementing vigorous family planning programs, and there will be corresponding differentials in fertility change. Among countries with identical declines in age-specific marital fertility rates, it is a mathematical necessity that countries with smaller proportions married will experience smaller TFR declines. In this situation, because countries with smaller proportions married will tend to have less vigorous programs, if an empirical indicator of marital composition is not explicitly included in the analysis, the TFR change which should be attributed to the causally prior differential in marital composition will instead be allocated, inappropriately, to the independent program effect.

In the present research, the socioeconomic indicators may reduce, to some extent, the magnitude of the marital composition bias in the program effect estimates, because these indicators can be related for various reasons to cross-national differentials in marital status composition. However, it is unlikely that the entire marital composition effect is adequately measured by the socioeconomic indicators, and since the marital composition might influence the magnitude of the program effort that can and will be mounted, the lack of a marital composition indicator, as well as the inability to fully measure every other relevant aspect of the socioeconomic setting, tends to lead to estimates of the independent program effect that are overestimates of the actual effect for the countries and time period studied.

Second, as discussed elsewhere (Demeny, 1979a; 1979b; Hernandez, 1981b), the measure of family planning program effort used here, and by Mauldin and Berelson (1978a) and Tsui and Bogue (1978), tends to produce biased results when the aim is to estimate the net program effect. The program effort index is derived from the 15 indicators listed in Table 18. Problems are associated with seven of these indicators. First, indicators numbered 3, 4, 10, and 11 appear to measure to some (possibly large) degree the commercial availability of contraception outside the organized family planning programs. In addition, because indicators numbered 4, 10, and 11 reflect in part the legality of birth control methods, high scores on these indicators may be, to an important degree, prerequisites to the implementation of organized family planning programs that offer a full complement of birth control methods.

**Table 18**
**Indicators of Family Planning Program Effort**

---

1.  Fertility reduction included in official planning policy

2.  Favorable public statements by political leaders

3.  Contraception readily and easily available, publicly and commercially throughout the country

4.  Customs and legal regulations allow importation of contraceptives not manufactured locally

5.  Vigorous effort to provide family planning services to all MWRA (Married Women of Reproductive Age)

6.  Adequate family planning administration structure

7.  Training facilities available and utilized

8.  Full-time home-visiting field workers

9.  Postpartum information, education, and service program

10. Abortion services openly and legally available to all

11. Voluntary sterilization services (male and female) openly and legally available to all

12. Use of mass media on a substantial basis

13. Government provides substantial part of family planning budget from its own resources

14. Record keeping systems for clients at clinic level and program service statistics

15. Serious and continuous evaluation effort

---

Source:  Mauldin and Berelson (1978a:  102).

Thus, the program effort index explicitly includes variation in the nonprogram provision of birth control methods and variation in the nonprogram political context which may precede or be necessary to the implementation of organized family planning programs. Insofar as this is the case, and insofar as these effects are not also captured by the socioeconomic indicators in a particular model, the contribution of these program effort indicators leads to an underestimate of the indigenous effect and to an overestimate of the independent program effect.

Another difficulty with the program effort index is that the indicators numbered 1, 2, and 13 may follow from fertility declines rather than produce them (Demeny, 1979a; 1979b). For example, political leaders may, in many cases, promulgate public statements favorable to family planning only after fertility has begun to decline and after birth control methods are commercially available, because only then do such statements pose relatively few political risks. Insofar as these political activities follow rather than lead fertility declines, and insofar as they are not encompassed in the socioeconomic indicators in a particular model, their contribution to the program strength index leads to an underestimated indigenous effect and an exaggerated estimate of the independent program effect.

On the other hand, it can be argued that several of these indicators should be included in the program index because of the possibility of a spillover effect. As discussed in Chapter 1, an organized family planning program might affect fertility not only by actually providing birth control methods to women but also by influencing additional women, perhaps through a mass media campaign, to adopt birth control methods that they obtain from nonprogram sources. Consequently, an index of program effort should incorporate indicators of the magnitude of the spillover effect. Indicators numbered 2, 3, 4, 6, 7, 8, 10, 11, and 14 have been conceived and employed in this fashion in a study by Srikantan (1977) which defines them as program inputs that might influence nonprogram birth control and hence fertility.

Unfortunately, four of these nine indicators lead to biased estimates of a program spillover effect. As discussed above, indicators numbered 4, 10, and 11 reflect in part the preprogram favorability of the legal context for the implementation of a program, and indicator number 2 may be strongly influenced by preprogram fertility circumstances. To the extent that this is true, these indicators appear to be beyond the influence of a family planning program and nearly one-half of the spillover indicators introduce a bias that leads to an underestimated indigenous effect and an exaggerated estimate of the net program effect.

In short, in the 15-indicator index of family planning program effort, between one-third and one-half of the indicators measure, to some extent, either prerequisites to the implementation of organized family planning programs or factors that follow rather than lead to fertility declines. As a result, the family planning program index tends to exaggerate the effect of the programs at the macro-level.

For all of these reasons, the 10 percent estimate of the independent program effect is likely to be an overestimate and, hence, can be considered an *upper limit* estimate of the actual independent program effect. In response to these difficulties, attention turns to arguments that provide the foundation for an alternative estimate of the independent program effect which can be viewed as a *lower limit* estimate.

Recall from Chapter 8 that the accuracy of the estimates from analytical strategy #5 rests upon the assumption that fertility at time 1 does not influence the socioeconomic setting as of the date to which the socioeconomic indicators refer. But it is possible that the earlier fertility level does have an impact on the socioeconomic setting at a later date, which in turn influences the magnitude of subsequent fertility change. If so, then part of the covariation between fertility at time 1 and fertility at time 2, which is eliminated in analytical strategy #5 from the estimate of the total socioeconomic effect, should be reintroduced, leading to an increased estimate.

In addition, Demeny (1979b: 500) has argued that in about a dozen countries a high level of program effort appears to be dependent on "prior fertility decline—that is, on a prior manifestation of effective demand for fertility control." If this is the case, then in the present empirical context fertility at time 1 influences the magnitude of the program effort and, through program effort, subsequent fertility. Hence, the entire covariation between fertility at time 1 and fertility at time 2 should not be excluded from consideration in estimating the socioeconomic effect, as it is in analytical strategy #5.

Finally, it also can be argued that the socioeconomic effect on fertility change does not occur with a time lag of precisely five or seven years, as is assumed in the present empirical estimates using strategy #5. Instead, fertility change may be influenced by the socioeconomic setting over a period spanning five to fifteen years or more. If this is the case, then adequate estimates of the socioeconomic effect require the introduction of one or more additional indicators that reflect variation in the socioeconomic context at an earlier date. One such "socioeconomic" indicator could be the variation in fertility at time 1, because it is influenced by and reflects socioeconomic factors prior to time 1. But as noted above, the covariation between fertility at time 1 and fertility at time 2 has been excluded from consideration in analytical strategy #5.

In short, each of these three arguments can be seen as calling for an analytical strategy which does not eliminate the entire covariation between fertility at time 1 and fertility at time 2 from the estimate of the socioeconomic effect, but which, instead, allocates at least some of this covariation to the socioeconomic setting, and hence to fertility change. This will lead, compared to the results from analytical strategy #5, to an increased estimate of the socioeconomic effect and a reduced estimate of the program effect.[4]

## DERIVING A RANGE OF ESTIMATES

How can these arguments be translated into alternative procedures for estimating the total socioeconomic and independent program effects? Recall that the calculations for deriving these estimates with analytical strategy #5 are:

$$\frac{\text{Socioeconomic}}{\text{Effect}} = \frac{(R_3^2 - r_1^2)}{(1.0 - r_1^2)} \qquad \frac{\text{Independent}}{\substack{\text{Program} \\ \text{Effect}}} = \frac{(R_4^2 - R_3^2)}{(1.0 - r_1^2)}$$

where,

$r_1^2$ = variation in fertility at time 2 that is accounted for by fertility at time 1;

$1.0 - r_1^2$ = variation in fertility at time 2 that is accounted for by fertility change;

$R_3^2$ = variation in fertility at time 2 that is accounted for by the socioeconomic indicators and fertility at time 1;

$R_3^2 - r_1^2$ = variation in fertility at time 2 that is accounted for by the socioeconomic indicators, independently of fertility at time 1;

$R_4^2$ = variation in fertility at time 2 that is accounted for by fertility at time 1, the socioeconomic indicators, and the family planning index;

$R_4^2 - R_3^2$ = variation in fertility at time 2 that is accounted for by the family planning index, independently of the socioeconomic indicators and fertility at time 1.

Now, all three of the arguments developed in the preceding section suggest that, although it is possible that fertility change between time 1 and time 2 is independent of the covariation between fertility at time 1 and fertility at time 2, part of this covariation may instead represent socioeconomic effects on fertility change, and, if so, then this part of the covariation should be included in the estimates of the socioeconomic effect and of fertility change.

Translated into mathematical terms, in the numerator of the formula above for the total socioeconomic effect, at least part of the value of $r_1^2$ should not be subtracted from $R_3^2$ to estimate the variation in fertility at time 2 that is accounted for by the socioeconomic setting. And in the denominator of the formulas for both the total socioeconomic effect and the family planning effect, at least part of the value of $r_1^2$ should not be subtracted from 1.0 to estimate the variation in fertility at time 2 that is accounted for by fertility change.

At the limit, these arguments imply that all of the covariation between fertility at time 1 and fertility at time 2 represents socioeconomic effects on fertility change, and hence all of the covariation represents fertility change. Mathematically, this is equivalent to setting $r_1^2$ equal to zero in both of the formulas above, which produces the following estimating formulas:

$$\frac{\text{Socioeconomic}}{\text{Effect}} = R_3^2 \qquad \frac{\text{Independent}}{\text{Program}}_{\text{Effect}} = R_4^2 - R_3^2$$

But these formulas are identical to the ones used to calculate the corresponding effects in analytical strategy #2. Consequently, the results in Tables 16 and 17 from analytical strategy #2 provide, as an alternative to the results from strategy #5, a set of estimates based on assumptions that take seriously the difficulties associated with analytical strategy #5.

In the present empirical context, this strategy may tend to overestimate the socioeconomic effect and underestimate the program effect, because the variation in fertility as measured at time 1 may be the result, in part, of an earlier independent program effect. Any such bias would be small to negligible, however, because a relatively small proportion of the third world countries included in the present analysis had implemented family planning programs before time 1, that is, before 1965 or 1968 depending on the fertility measure employed.[5]

Hence, the results from strategy #2 provide a plausible upper limit to the percentage of the variation in fertility change, during the late 1960s and early 1970s for the 83 third world countries studied, that is accounted for by the socioeconomic setting, and they provide a plausible lower limit to the independent program effect for these countries during this period (see Appendix for a list of the countries).

Taking into consideration all the arguments presented in this and the preceding chapters, it appears that, independently of the socioeconomic setting, family planning programs account for between 3 percent and 10 percent of the variation in fertility change during the late 1960s and early 1970s for the 83 countries studied. It should not be forgotten, however, that this range also may overestimate the program effect, because the strategy for calculating the lower end of the range may still fail to capture all the relevant features of the socioeconomic setting, and it may not fully eliminate the biases introduced by the program effort index.[6]

## CONCLUSIONS

Deficiencies in past cross-national studies dominate the recent debate concerning the independent impact of family planning programs on fertility in third world countries. Drawing on this and additional theoretical and methodological literature, the present cross-national study derives a more firmly grounded estimate of the independent program effect by delineating the relevant macro-level theoretical arguments, by evaluating the adequacy of potentially appropriate analytical strategies, and by implementing these strategies with data compiled for the earlier studies. This analysis also provided an opportunity to pursue again the question addressed by Entwisle (1981) regarding the relative adequacy of the CBR and TFR for cross-national studies of fertility.

Contrary to the results obtained by Entwisle (1981), the new results obtained here indicate that parallel analyses with the CBR and TFR sometimes produce conclusions that are quite similar, but in other cases the conclusions are quite different. Whether or not the results are similar or different depends on the analytical purpose, the analytical strategy, and the empirical indicators included in a particular research effort.

Turning to the primary purpose of the present research, if all of the arguments and results presented in this and the preceding chapters are taken into consideration, the best estimate is that, independently of the socioeconomic setting, family planning programs account for between 3 percent and 10 percent of cross-national variation in fertility change during the late 1960s and early 1970s for the 83 third world countries studied. This estimate is substantially smaller than both the 15 percent to 20 percent suggested by the analysis of Mauldin and Berelson (1978a) and the 19 percent suggested by the analysis of Tsui and Bogue (1978), although it is possible that this new estimate also is too large.

As discussed in Chapter 8, because these new results were obtained through cross-national analyses of national-level data, their theoretical interpretation lies in the realm of national socioeconomic structures and processes, aggregate demographic change, and family planning programs as instruments of national and international policy. Within this theoretical context, the independent program effect refers to the extent to which differences in fertility change across third world countries are accounted for, not by differences in the socioeconomic settings of these countries, but instead either by differences in the proactive initiatives of political leaders in these countries or by differences in the proactive initiatives of donor agencies, international agencies, governments of developed countries, or other factors external to the third world countries themselves.

In view of this theoretical interpretation, the relatively small magnitude of the new estimates of the independent program effect suggests that, in pursuing family planning policies that have differentially influenced fertility trends, political leaders in third world countries were responding primarily to internal socioeconomic conditions rather than acting either on their independent perceptions of the need for such programs or on independent information, encouragement, and pressure from extra-national agencies. In short, these results suggest that, during the late 1960s and early 1970s for the 83 third world countries studied, insofar as the purpose was to produce fertility declines greater than the declines that might be expected to flow from the socioeconomic setting, family planning programs had little independent effect as instruments of national and international policy (see Appendix for a list of the 83 countries).

## NOTES

1. The data published by Tsui and Bogue (1978) differ in a substantial number of cases from the data presented in the sources they cite. Where discrepancies occur, data from the sources cited by Tsui and Bogue are used in the new calculations of the present research.

2. "Pace of Social Change" and "1970 Population Density" are each included as separate independent variables. "Island-status" is included as two dummy variables reflecting "Island" and "Quasi-Island" statuses. See Mauldin and Berelson (1978a), Cleland and Singh (1980), and Hernandez (1981b) for discussions of reasons for including these indicators.

3. Data measuring literacy are obtained from Mauldin and Berelson (1978a) instead of from Tsui and Bogue (1978), because in the latter study data are missing for about one-third of the countries studied here.

4. The arguments developed in this section also apply to the analysis of CBR change.

5. Based on information provided by Nortman (1975b: 32–35), before 1965 only 3 of the 83 countries included in the present analysis had antinatalist policies, while 1 additional country offered meaningful support for a family planning program on other than demographic grounds. By 1967 these figures had increased to 13 and 4. The small to negligible size of any associated bias is also suggested by the following. Such a bias would tend to exaggerate a socioeconomic effect estimate based on the TFR more than one based on the CBR, because analyses based on the TFR start at a later date (1968 instead of 1965) after a larger number of countries had initiated family planning programs. But empirically the reverse occurred. The best socioeconomic effect estimate based on strategy #2 and the TFR is actually smaller than the corresponding estimate derived with the CBR. Similarly, such a bias would for the same reason lead to more of an underestimate of the program effect for an analysis based on the TFR than for one based on the CBR. But the best program effect estimates based on the TFR and the CBR are identical when strategy #2 is employed. Both suggest that 3 percent of the variation in fertility change is an independent program effect.

6. Additional features of the socioeconomic setting that may be relevant, but which are not explicitly incorporated into the present analysis, include energy consumption, the extent to which the transportation network is de-

veloped, and the extent to which the mass media permeate society. Although measurement error in the program effort index may tend to lead to an underestimate of the independent program effect, any such bias is probably slight compared to the countervailing bias, mentioned above, that is associated with between one-third and one-half of the indicators constituting the program effort index. The Appendix lists the 83 countries included in the new cross-national analysis presented here.

# 10

# Past Program Performance and Future Policy Implications

The primary purpose of this monograph has been to determine whether family planning programs have been a success or a failure as an independent policy initiative in reducing fertility and hence population growth in the third world. Statistics presented in Chapter 1 suggest that these programs have achieved considerable success in their most immediate goal—the provision of supplies, services, and information about modern birth control methods to individuals. But these statistics provide no information about whether this apparent success in providing birth control methods and information was, in fact, driven by socioeconomic and other indigenous forces. In other words, these statistics by themselves indicate nothing about whether the fertility declines in third world countries occurred because of independent program initiatives or because of socioeconomic conditions or changes that are known to influence both program effort and fertility through a variety of mechanisms. It is this question about the net effect on fertility of family planning programs as an independent policy initiative that has been the subject of continuing scientific controversy and the primary focus of this monograph.

Three kinds of evidence have been developed and presented here in seeking to answer this question for the period spanning the mid–1960s to the mid–1970s—the period during which family planning programs were widely adopted, but prior to which such programs were augmented with major policy efforts relying upon incentives, disincentives, and political pressures of various types. First, in order to resolve inconsistencies in the conclusions drawn from past research, Chapter 2 employs a general conceptual model to ascertain the nature and direction of biases inherent in the research designs of past studies. Then Chapters 3 through 7 utilize the best available research design to study four countries which many observers believe have implemented relatively successful family planning programs. Finally, Chapters 8 and 9 implement the best available cross-national research design to evaluate the success of family planning programs for 83 third world countries. The present chapter briefly summarizes the major conclusions from these diverse sets of evidence, and then discusses implications of these conclusions for the future development of successful policies to reduce fertility in the third world.

## THE EVIDENCE FROM PAST RESEARCH

Past studies have used five major types of research designs in assessing the independent impact of family planning programs in third world countries. Key distinguishing features are whether fertility is measured before and after the program is implemented, and how many times; whether a control group and/or statistical controls are employed; and whether individual women or geographical areas are used as the unit of analysis.

Lacking a control group and using individuals as the unit of analysis, studies using the one-group pretest-posttest design are flawed by each of the four classes of bias—history, maturation, self-selection, and statistical regression—leading to exaggerated estimates of the net program effect. Research using the nonequivalent control group design with individuals as the unit of analysis eliminates two of these biases—history and maturation—by incorporating a control group into the analysis, but the problems of self-selection and statistical regression remain to exaggerate the net program effect.

A shift from individuals to geographic areas as the unit of analysis in the nonequivalent control group design eliminates the statistical regression bias in six of the studies discussed here, but self-selection remains a problem. A second set of studies that also eliminates all the biases except self-selection relies upon the posttest-only control group design which includes both an experimental and a control group but which measures fertility only after the program has been implemented. As in the research discussed above, the self-selection biases in these studies lead to overestimates of the net program effect, because all causes of differential fertility change are confounded with program activities.

An alternative design strategy that eliminates all but one kind of bias involves measuring fertility several times before and after the program is implemented with geographic areas as the unit of analysis. In this interrupted time series design, self-selection and statistical regression are eliminated by studying the entire population of a country with a family planning program, and maturation is eliminated as a problem by using the preprogram trend in fertility as a means of measuring the effect of maturational changes. This strategy also reduces the bias from history to the extent that historical shifts in social, economic, and other conditions of the country studied are steady and gradual, as opposed to irregular or discontinuous. One additional study expanded the interrupted time series design by adding a control country with a time series of fertility measurements. This control series design formally eliminates the history bias by taking account of the effects of history as they are manifest in the control country.

Although a few of these studies focus on the independent program effect across a substantial number of third world countries, most focus on a single country. Studies using the best research designs—the interrupted time series and control series designs—have assessed the net program effect for the countries of Hong Kong, Singapore, and Taiwan. The critical evaluation in Chapter 2 indicated that the best study of Hong Kong was conducted by Wat and Hodge (1972), who found no decisive empirical evidence that family planning program activities were an independent causal factor in Hong Kong's fertility decline. The two studies of Singapore by Wolfers (1970) and by Chang and Hauser (1975) did find an independent program effect, but an analysis which extends these studies to encompass a few more years indicates that much of this effect was transitory and the longer-term effect was small. Finally, the best studies of Taiwan, which were conducted by Davis (1967) and Li (1973), found that the family planning program had little, if any, independent effect on fertility.

Overall, then, this broad-brush evaluation of past research suggests that various studies draw different, sometimes contradictory, conclusions because they rely upon different research designs and hence different kinds of evidence. To make sense of these inconsistencies the approach taken in Chapter 2 is to ascertain the nature, number, and direction of biases that are associated with various studies by virtue of the types of research designs and units of analysis which they employ. This critical evaluation shows that differences in results are associated with the differential validity of various studies, and that the least biased studies find little or no net program effects. The insights gained from this analysis were then used as the foundation for deriving new estimates in case studies of four third world countries and in a cross-national study of 83 third world countries.

## THE EVIDENCE FROM NEW CASE STUDIES

The new case studies of Taiwan, South Korea, Costa Rica, and Mauritius which were developed in Chapters 3 through 7 rely upon the best research design that can be implemented for all four countries with available data—the interrupted time series design. Although the control series design is more adequate in a formal methodological sense, the use of the control series design is precluded in the present research by the lack of control countries which experienced historical conditions and changes similar to each of the four countries of primary interest. The interrupted time series design that is used here instead consists of two stages which, taken together, allocate CBR change after program implementation either to the program, as an independent policy initiative, or to various socioeconomic, demographic, and related factors.

The first stage of the analysis decomposes CBR change into components measuring the effects of change in the age-sex and marital status compositions and change in age-specific marital fertility rates. The age-sex effects for these countries, which result from socioeconomic and related factors that influence demographic change, range in magnitude from small (1 percent to 4 percent) in Taiwan, Costa Rica, and Mauritius to substantial (23 percent to 25 percent) in South Korea. The marital status effects vary even more from small but negative in Costa Rica ( − 3 percent), to moderate in Taiwan (10 percent), to substantial in South Korea (20 percent to 23 percent) and Mauritius (33 percent). The marital status composition effects result from nonprogram indigenous factors such as socioeconomic changes, including rising education and rising female employment in the nonagricultural sector, which can foster increases in age at marriage.

The second stage of the analysis focuses on change in age-specific marital fertility rates which can result either from indigenous causes or from the family planning program as an independent policy initiative. This interrupted time series approach utilizes preprogram fertility trends to develop projections of subsequent fertility levels which might have been expected in the absence of family planning programs. The procedure assumes that, if the program had not been introduced, the kind of fertility change occurring prior to the program would have continued.

Since fertility change prior to the program resulted from changing family size goals, changing availability of birth control, and involuntary fertility change, this assumption suggests that these nonprogram causes would have continued in combination to produce the same sort of fertility decline that they produced prior to program implementation. Furthermore, since these three factors are in turn influenced by a wide variety of socioeconomic and other indigenous forces, the assumption also suggests that socioeconomic and other indigenous factors would have continued through various mechanisms to have produced the same sort of fertility change that they produced prior to the program.

Although the correctness of these assumptions cannot be known with absolute certainty, specific projection assumptions were derived based on (1) assessments for each country of the nature of change in key socioeconomic indicators prior to and following program implementation, (2) assessments for each country of the nature of preprogram fertility change, and (3) expectations of demographers who have attended to the nature of fertility change in countries undergoing socioeconomic development. When warranted by these assessments, expectations, and the quality of available fertility data, projections were derived assuming a continuation of accelerating fertility change. In other circumstances, simpler more conservative assumptions of continuing linear change were employed, or a range of assumptions and estimates were developed.

The results based on these procedures for Taiwan and South Korea are the most adequate. They indicate that about 11 percent of the Taiwanese CBR decline during 1964–1975 and about 1 percent to 10 percent of the South Korean CBR decline during 1965–1971 were net effects of the family planning programs in these countries. Less adequate are the results for Costa Rica which suggest that between 4 percent and 23 percent, but probably closer to 4 percent, of the CBR decline during 1967–1971 is a net program effect. Finally, considerably less adequate are the results for Mauritius which suggest that between 34 percent and 51 percent of the CBR decline during 1965–1975 was a net program effect, although the relatively lengthy chain of reasoning required to derive this range suggests that the results should be interpreted with considerable caution.

Combining the results from these analyses of marital fertility trends with the results from the first stage, which pertains to the effects of change in the age-sex and marital status compositions, produces the following conclusions about the role of socioeconomic, demographic, and other indigenous factors in the fertility declines of these four countries. The results for Mauritius, which it should be noted again must be interpreted with considerable caution, suggest that between 49 percent and 66 percent of the CBR decline during 1965–1975 was due to indigenous factors that led to declines in the proportion married among younger women and declines in marital fertility among women in the prime childbearing ages. The socioeconomic mechanism that appears most important here is that rising socioeconomic aspirations, reflected in rising educational attainments, were forestalled by a lack of economic growth.

Much more adequate are the results for Costa Rica which suggest that between 77 percent and 96 percent, but probably closer to 96 percent, of the CBR decline during 1967–1971 was due to indigenous factors which led to declines in marital fertility among women in the prime childbearing ages. These fertility declines occurred during a period of accelerating socioeconomic change, at least as reflected in indicators related to educational achievements, the occupational distribution, and per capita GNP. The most adequate results are for Taiwan and South Korea. In Taiwan about 89 percent of the CBR decline during 1964–1975 was due to indigenous causes, and in South Korea between 90 percent and 99 percent of the CBR decline during 1965–1971 was due to indigenous causes. Although some of this effect for South Korea is due to age-sex composition change, most of the indigenous effects for both Taiwan and South Korea are due to declines in the proportion married among younger women and declines in marital fertility among older women. Taiwan and South Korea are, of course, leading examples of economic success stories among third world countries in Asia, and this success apparently accounts for most of the substantial fertility declines in these countries.

## THE EVIDENCE FROM NEW CROSS-NATIONAL RESEARCH

The new cross-national study of 83 third world countries developed in Chapters 8 and 9 relies upon the best research design that can be implemented for such a large number of third world countries—the nonequivalent control group design. Although the interrupted time series and control series designs are more adequate in a formal methodological sense, the use of these designs is precluded in the present research by the lack for many third world countries of reliable, extended time series data measuring fertility and socioeconomic conditions. However, in order to insure that the conclusions drawn from the nonequivalent control group design adopted here suffer the least possible bias, Chapters 8 and 9 merge six different methodological inquiries to provide a firm foundation for deriving empirical results, and they delineate the precise nature of macro-theoretical conclusions that can be drawn from the cross-national analysis.

One of the six methodological inquiries is an evaluation of five distinct analytical strategies that provide plausible approaches for deriving empirical estimates of the total socioeconomic and independent program effects. Each of these five strategies is based upon either the nonequivalent control group design or the posttest-only control group design. A second methodological inquiry provides means for reducing the magnitude of major biases in these research designs, namely self-selection biases. A third inquiry provides theoretical and mathematical means for avoiding the problem of multicollinearity which can be associated with analyzing highly correlated variables. A fourth inquiry, which concerns the index of family planning program effort that has been employed in major cross-national studies, including the present one, identifies biases associated with using this index when the aim is to estimate the independent program effect. This inquiry also provides means for reducing these program index biases.

A fifth methodological inquiry uses theoretical, mathematical, and empirical arguments to compare results derived with the CBR to results derived with the TFR. These arguments suggest that independent program effect estimates derived with the TFR are more adequate, because they are not artificially inflated by the causally prior effect that change in the age-sex composition can have on both family planning programs and CBR change. Finally, the sixth methodological inquiry draws upon the previous five and upon additional arguments, including the possible confounding of the causally prior effect that change in the marital status composition can have on both family planning programs and fertility, to derive a range of estimates of the independent program effect and the total socioeconomic effect.

Beyond these six methodological inquiries, the cross-national research in Chapters 8 and 9 also relies upon a macro-theoretical analysis of the determinants of cross-national variation in aggregate fertility change. From this perspective, the total socioeconomic effect refers to cross-national variation in aggregate fertility change that is due to cross-national variation in socioeconomic settings and other indigenous factors. Two components can be distinguished. First, the direct socioeconomic effect reflects cross-national variation in the demand for and use of nonprogram means of limiting births. Second, the indirect socioeconomic effect reflects cross-national variation not only in the indigenous demand for program supplied birth control methods, but also in the infrastructure and sociopolitical context that influence the extent to which family planning programs can and will be implemented by governments in third world countries. The independent program effect, in contrast, refers to the cross-national variation in aggregate fertility change that is due either to the proactive initiatives of governments in third world countries or to the responses of these governments to information, encouragement, or pressure from extra-national agencies, such as foreign donors, insofar as these are independent of cross-national variation in socioeconomic settings.

Results founded upon these methodological and theoretical arguments indicate that family planning programs account for between 3 percent and 10 percent of the cross-national variation in fertility change during the late 1960s and early 1970s for the 83 third world countries studied, independent of cross-national variation in socioeconomic and other indigenous conditions. The remaining cross-national variation in fertility change that was the result of cross-national variation in socioeconomic and other indigenous factors is associated with (1) the demand for means of limiting births, (2) the transportation, communications, and administrative/bureaucratic infrastructures which influence the magnitude of program effort that can be mounted in different countries, and (3) indigenous sociopolitical factors that influence the extent to which governments are willing to implement family planning programs.

## CONCLUSIONS AND IMPLICATIONS FOR FUTURE POLICY SUCCESS

Statistics measuring knowledge and use of modern birth control methods in third world countries suggest that many family planning programs have achieved considerable success in providing individuals with information about and access to such methods, but additional evidence presented in this monograph suggests that, as a policy initiative independent of socioeconomic and other indigenous conditions, family planning programs had relatively little impact on fertility during the late 1960s and early 1970s. Modern contraceptive usage rates in third world countries, while substantial, remain generally below usage rates in developed countries, and much of the fertility decline that appears to have been effected through program supplied methods was a consequence of changes in socioeconomic conditions and other indigenous factors.

To be more specific, the major empirical conclusions of this monograph, which are based on extensive studies of individual third world countries and on cross-national research for 83 third world countries, can be summarized as follows. The most adequate case studies of individual countries, as identified in the critical evaluation of past research or as developed here, encompass six countries which many observers believe have implemented relatively successful family planning programs. Only for one of these countries, Mauritius, is the estimated magnitude of the net program effect as large as one-third to one-half of the CBR decline, but for methodological reasons this estimate must be interpreted with considerable caution. The much more adequate results for Costa Rica, Hong Kong, Singapore, South Korea, and Taiwan suggest that, although a net program effect on the order of 20 percent of recent fertility declines is possible in one or two cases, more probable are program effect estimates on the order of 10 percent or less for periods spanning five to ten years. The new cross-national research leads to similar conclusions. Perhaps as much as 10 percent but possibly as little as 3 percent of the cross-national variation in fertility change in the third world during the late 1960s and early 1970s was an independent effect of family planning programs.

In other words, most of the fertility change that occurred within and across the third world countries studied here, and hence much of the immediate success of family planning programs in providing birth control information, supplies, and services, appears to have been produced by a variety of indigenous factors, but particularly by socioeconomic conditions and changes. These are the same sort of factors that produced major fertility declines historically, in the face of government opposition to birth control methods, during the early Industrial Revolution in the developed countries, and they produced important fertility declines that began more recently, but prior to the implementation of government-supported national family planning programs, in various third world countries.

Consequently, the research reviewed and conducted here implies the following conclusion about the success or failure of family planning programs for the third world countries and the time period studied. Notwithstanding the apparent success of these programs in facilitating fertility declines through the provision of information about and access to modern birth control methods, insofar as the ultimate goal of government-supported national family planning programs in third world countries has been to initiate major fertility reductions that are independent of other fertility determinants, these programs have experienced little success and considerable failure.

What are the implications for the development of fertility reduction policies that will be successful in the future? The answer to this question depends partly on judgments about the magnitude of future fertility reductions that need to be brought about through new policy initiatives. That is, the answer depends partly on judgments about likely future trends in fertility and population growth in the absence of major changes in current conditions and policies, and about the likely consequences of these trends for human welfare. Although detailed judgments on these matters are beyond the scope of this monograph, the following can be offered to provide some basis for discussing implications of the present research for future fertility reduction policies.

First, as noted in Chapter 1, the United Nations (1981) estimates that with a CBR decline of about 20 percent between 1960–1965 and 1975–1980, the population of the third world expanded dramatically from 2.1 billion to 3.3 billion people. Looking to the next twenty years, assuming that current trends and policies continue and that the CBR will decline by another 20 percent, the United Nations (1981) medium projection suggests that the third world will continue to expand dramatically by an additional 1.5 billion people to reach 4.8 billion by the year 2000. Although this projection is not intended as a prediction, if this population growth actually occurs, and if important new poverty reduction policies are not implemented, it is difficult to imagine that poverty and deprivation will not increase in many third world countries during the coming decades. Insofar as expanded public policies to reduce fertility are judged necessary to insure that such population growth and increasing poverty do not occur, the present research has the following implications for the development of successful fertility reduction policies in the future.

Despite the value of family planning programs in providing birth control technology that facilitates fertility declines driven by other forces, these programs will not by themselves bring about major fertility reductions of the required magnitude. Hence, current family planning programs should be augmented with new fertility reduction policies directed toward the underlying determinants of fertility, policies that directly confront the issue of individual reproductive motivation. The research presented here suggests, based on contemporary fertility declines, that such policies should focus on socioeconomic conditions and socioeconomic change. In addition, drawing upon earlier recommendations by other scholars who have studied the determinants of historical and contemporary fertility declines, and drawing upon descriptions of recent policy initiatives in several third world countries in Asia, Chapter 1 presented a wide variety of policies that might be adopted to augment existing family planning programs. Such policies also directly confront, although in quite diverse ways, the issue of individual reproductive motivation.

Four analytically distinct types of policies can be distinguished: socioeconomic development policies, positive socioeconomic incentives, negative socioeconomic incentives, and policies involving direct sociopolitical pressure or coercion. As suggested by the U.N. World Population Plan of Action and by various scholars, criteria for selecting one socioeconomic development policy in preference to another might include not only the magnitude of expected economic growth and improvements in human welfare, but also the magnitude of expected fertility declines. More directly linked to fertility behavior, positive socioeconomic incentives, such as low-interest loans and mechanical cultivators, might be offered explicitly in return for the achievement of fertility goals. Also directly linked to fertility behavior, negative socioeconomic incentives might involve the withdrawal of existing benefits, such as privileged access to public housing, explicitly in response to a failure to achieve fertility reduction goals. Finally, fertility goals might be achieved by applying direct pressure through sociopolitical institutions or by applying coercive measures, such as forced abortion or sterilization.

What criteria, in addition to effectiveness in reducing fertility, should be utilized in the future to evaluate and select among these four potentially successful, but quite different, policy approaches to reducing fertility?[1] Although a detailed answer to this question is beyond the scope of this monograph, partly because such decisions clearly rest with third world countries themselves, two criteria that might be considered in such deliberations can be suggested here briefly in closing, namely the differential effects of alternative policies on human welfare and on human freedom.[2]

## POTENTIAL POLICIES, HUMAN WELFARE, AND HUMAN FREEDOM

Alternative fertility reduction policies may have a variety of indirect and direct consequences for human welfare and freedom. Indirect consequences may include the following. First, insofar as the rapid population growth associated with high fertility leads to reductions in human welfare, any policy that produces a decline in fertility, and hence a decline in population growth, will tend indirectly, through these mechanisms, to enhance human welfare. Second, insofar as local community pressures compel individuals to bear substantial numbers of children, any policy that produces fertility decline will tend indirectly, as a consequence, to enhance individual freedom by counterbalancing prior limits on the range of effective individual choices that were enforced by local community pressures. Third, insofar as rapid population growth leads to constrictions in the range of human freedoms, any policy that produces fertility decline will tend indirectly, as a result, to forestall future reductions in the range of human freedoms.[3]

Turning to the direct consequences of fertility reduction policies, socioeconomic development policies and positive socioeconomic incentives will tend (1) to directly improve human welfare by providing new socioeconomic benefits, and (2) to directly enhance human freedom by providing new socioeconomic choices. However, negative socioeconomic incentives and policies of sociopolitical pressure and coercion will tend (1) to directly reduce welfare insofar as existing socioeconomic benefits are withdrawn, and (2) to directly reduce freedom insofar as individual reproductive choices are circumscribed or thwarted.

In short, these arguments suggest that all four major types of policies will tend to enhance welfare and freedom indirectly by reducing fertility and population growth. Socioeconomic development policies and positive socioeconomic incentives also will tend to enhance welfare and freedom directly by providing new benefits and choices. But negative socioeconomic incentives and sociopolitical pressure and coercion will tend to directly reduce welfare and freedom. Considering all four types of policies, then, insofar as human welfare and freedom are valued, socioeconomic development policies and positive socioeconomic incentives would appear to be preferable.

Among the four countries which have implemented fertility reduction policies that augment the family planning approach,[4] only Thailand appears to be relying upon positive incentives without also utilizing negative incentives or sociopolitical pressures. Singapore is relying upon both positive and negative incentives. Indonesia is relying upon sociopolitical pressure and, more recently, upon positive incentives. China is relying upon a uniquely wide range of positive incentives, negative incentives, and sociopolitical pressures. The breadth and intensity of these policy measures suggest that the governments of these countries are deeply concerned about the harmful consequences which they believe would follow from rapid population growth in the absence of fertility reduction efforts that augment substantially the family planning approach which relies primarily upon providing birth control information and services.

Will future fertility reduction policies in these and other third world countries emphasize socioeconomic development and positive incentives, or are they more likely to emphasize negative incentives and political pressure or coercion? Using presently available socioeconomic resources, third world countries might redirect existing efforts toward specific policy initiatives that appear especially likely to foster fertility declines. It is possible that such redirected policy efforts, utilizing existing resources to fund alternative types of socioeconomic development or positive incentives, would experience considerable success in reducing fertility.

But it should not be forgotten that the primary rationale for pursuing fertility reduction policies is to facilitate socioeconomic development in the face of scarce resources. Precisely because of severe constraints on the current availability of socioeconomic resources in third world countries, it seems likely that many of them, but particularly the poorest, will be quite limited in their ability either to expand existing socioeconomic development programs or to initiate new positive incentive programs. Consequently, insofar as the fertility declines that can be brought about by redirecting existing resources are judged by third world countries to be inadequate, they may feel a need to pursue policies which rely upon negative incentives or political pressures to achieve fertility reduction goals.

Many third world countries currently fund programs which provide socioeconomic benefits that could be withdrawn in conjunction with a negative incentive program, but these benefits may be small in magnitude, limited in coverage, and/or concerned with the most basic of human needs, such as nutrition. Consequently, benefit programs which are required to implement large scale negative incentive policies are lacking in many third world countries, and the use of existing benefits in such efforts might lead in some cases to rather direct and immediate reductions in human welfare. Such difficulties can severely limit the ability of third world countries to implement negative incentive policies that are potentially effective in producing fertility declines.

The fourth and last major type of fertility reduction policy relies less directly upon socioeconomic resources, and may for this reason appear increasingly attractive in some third world countries. This approach relies, however, upon the presence of or possibility of creating strong and powerful sociopolitical organizations. The presence of such organizations varies greatly across third world countries, and although such a direct strategy for reducing fertility might be relatively successful in certain cases, the political risks in pursuing such a strategy are in many cases obvious and substantial.

What does all this suggest for successful fertility reduction policies in third world countries during future decades? The research reviewed and conducted here suggests that, although family planning programs have played an important role in facilitating fertility declines in third world countries, during the late 1960s and early 1970s these programs experienced little success and considerable failure in initiating fertility reductions independently of socioeconomic and other indigenous factors in these countries. In addition, despite significant fertility declines that were driven primarily by socioeconomic development and other nonprogram factors, the third world experienced unprecedented population growth.

Looking to the future and assuming a continuation of present trends and policies, fertility will continue to decline, but not enough to forestall an even greater increase in the population of the third world during the next twenty years. Socioeconomic and sociopolitical policies that redirect existing, currently available, resources to encourage further fertility declines appear to promise considerable success and might be adopted. But, again, it should not be forgotten that the magnitude of available socioeconomic resources in many of these countries, particularly the poorest countries, is relatively small. Consequently, although the marginal effects of such policies could be quite important, they might fall considerably short of the perceived need.

To the extent that this is true, and to the extent that third world governments view as desirable the expansion of such policies, but particularly socioeconomic development policies and positive socioeconomic incentives, which directly enhance welfare and freedom by providing new socioeconomic benefits and choices, these countries may require additional resources from outside the third world, that is, from the developed countries. Without major new initiatives in third world countries, and/or without corresponding changes in the international policies of the developed countries, the number of people suffering severe deprivation in third world countries may continually expand during the next twenty years as relatively high fertility levels produce continuing rapid population growth. In conclusion, the failures of past fertility reduction policies and the prospects for further unprecedented population growth confront third world countries, as well as developed countries, with momentous decisions that could fundamentally influence the poverty, welfare, and freedom experienced by billions of people around the world.

## NOTES

1. See Hernandez (1984) for a review of literature addressing ethical questions associated with selecting among a wide range of fertility reduction policies, and for a more detailed discussion of ethical questions that call for additional attention.

2. For a brief discussion of the full range of possible population policies see Hernandez (forthcoming).

3. See Davis (1975) for arguments suggesting that projected increases in population size and urbanization in Asia, if they occur, are likely to lead to increasingly totalitarian governments. See Hernandez (1984) for additional related research and for a more detailed discussion of the salient ethical issues.

4. Forced sterilization was used briefly in India, but it proved to be quite unpopular and apparently is no longer practiced. See Edmondson (1981) for an anthropological study of factors in Bali, Indonesia that influence both family planning program strength and fertility. See Tien (1984) for a discussion of how the population policy of China differs from the approach to family planning typically instituted in third world countries, and for a study of the effect of the Chinese policy and of socioeconomic change on fertility in China.

# Appendix

## POPULATION AND BIRTH ESTIMATES

All of the results from the decomposition analyses and projection analyses presented in Chapters 3 through 7 for the case studies of Taiwan, South Korea, Costa Rica, and Mauritius are derived using population data and birth data published in or estimated from the references cited in the text. This appendix identifies the basic population data and basic birth data that are estimated, and describes the procedures that are used to obtain these estimates.

First, whenever published data include a category of "age unknown," these data are allocated to various ages according to the distribution of published data for which the ages are known. Second, midyear age, sex, and marital status specific population estimates are derived, as needed, by linear interpolation from the two sets of census and/or registration data which are nearest in time and which bound the year(s) of interest, or by linear extrapolation from the two sets of census and/or registration data which are nearest in time to the years(s) of interest. Third, annual birth data specific for age and marital status of mother are derived, as needed, from these population data and estimates and from available age-specific fertility rate estimates. Decomposition results and projection results are derived with these data and estimates as discussed in the text.

## ADDITIONAL PROCEDURES FOR SOUTH KOREA

As mentioned in Chapter 5, because accurate birth data were not collected on a continuing basis for the period of interest, two sets of fertility estimates prepared by Cho (1973b: 275) and Moon et al. (1973: 120–123) are combined with census data to approximate the actual demographic situation in South Korea. Because of apparent errors and differences in these two sets of fertility estimates, procedures somewhat more complicated than the ones described above are employed for South Korea.

Moon et al. (1973) state that following the publication of their report on the 1971 fertility-abortion survey, it was discovered that the five peaks in the total fertility rate trend correspond to the thirteen month lunar leap years of 1960, 1963, 1966, 1968, 1971 (384 ± 1 days during leap years versus 354 ± 1 days during non-leap years). As a result, the fertility estimates from the 1971 fertility-abortion survey for these five years appear to be systematically and erroneously large compared to other years during the period. Therefore, using the CBR for 1964 as the initial year in the decomposition and the CBR for 1971 as the final year would probably produce distorted results.

The four peaks in the total fertility rate trend based on Cho's (1973b) estimates also correspond to the lunar leap years 1960, 1963, 1966, and 1968, suggesting that similar errors exist in these data. Using the CBR in 1964 as the initial year in the decomposition and the CBR for 1970, the most recent year for which Cho estimates the CBR, as the final year in the decomposition also might produce distorted results, since 1964 immediately follows but does not immediately precede a lunar leap year and 1970 immediately precedes but does not immediately follow a lunar leap year.

In order to minimize errors introduced by inaccuracies in the fertility-abortion survey estimates by Moon et al. and to analyze data for the most recent period possible, means are calculated from data for 1970 and 1971 and used as the final year for the decomposition. To insure maximum comparability between data for the final and initial dates, means are calculated from data for 1962 and 1963 and used as the initial year in the decomposition.

As noted above, fertility estimates for 1963 and 1971 are systematically erroneously large. Presumably, fertility estimates for 1962 and 1970, years immediately preceding lunar leap years, are systematically erroneously small. Furthermore, errors in the 1962 estimates compared to errors in the 1963 estimates and errors in the 1970 estimates compared to errors in the 1971 estimates are probably similar. Therefore, means of estimates for the two sets of dates, representing fertility for the years centered on January 1, 1963, and January 1, 1971, should be maximally comparable and minimally erroneous.

In order to take advantage of the fact that Cho (1973b) derived an alternative set of fertility estimates, but one which extended only through 1970, the following procedures also are employed. First, mean estimates based on Cho's data are used to derive a decomposition with initial and final years centered on January 1, 1963, and January 1, 1970. Second, a similar decomposition is derived from the fertility estimates of Moon et al. Then the differences between the decompositions based on estimates by Moon et al., which end on January 1, 1970, and January 1, 1971, are calculated and applied to the decomposition based on Cho's estimates to adjust it to the end-year of January 1, 1971. This produces decomposition results based on Cho's fertility estimates which are maximally comparable to the decomposition results based on the fertility estimates by Moon et al.

Errors in the fertility estimates by Moon et al. and by Cho also suggest the need for the special projection procedures in the analysis of age-specific marital fertility rates that are described next. First, to minimize the effect of the possible overestimation of fertility in 1960, 1963, 1966, 1968, and 1971 and the possible underestimation of fertility during the other years, two sets of mean estimated fertility rates are derived using data for 1960 and 1961 and for 1963 and 1964. Since the fertility estimates for 1960 and 1963 appear to be erroneously large, since the estimates for 1961 and 1964 presumably are erroneously small, and since the overestimates and underestimates for contiguous years are likely to be of about the same magnitude, the procedure relying upon two sets of mean estimates should lead to relatively unbiased results which are maximally comparable. The use of simple linear projections based on these estimates, which represent fertility in the years centered on January 1, 1961, and January 1, 1964, should produce relatively unbiased results.

In order to minimize error in estimated fertility between 1965 and 1971, mean fertility rates for each subset of two years are used in calculations involving the projected rates, all of which are centered on January 1 of the appropriate year, to obtain estimates of the net program effect.

In order to obtain net program effect estimates from Cho's fertility data that are comparable to the estimates from the fertility data provided by Moon et al., procedures are developed analogously to the ones discussed above for the decomposition procedure. Specifically, net program effects based on Cho's data are derived for the years January 1, 1966, through January 1, 1970, with procedures identical to the ones described in the two preceding paragraphs. Then projections are derived with these procedures from the data by Moon et al. for these same years, January 1, 1966, through January 1, 1970.

Next the differences between the two sets of net program effect estimates derived from data by Moon et al. for the years 1966–1970 and 1966–1971 are obtained. These differences then are applied to the results from Cho's data for the years 1966–1970 to adjust them to the years 1966–1971. These are the results presented in the text in Chapter 5.

## THE POPULATION GROWTH ASSUMPTION

As indicated above, the basic assumption underlying all of the population estimates derived here for specific years is that population growth occurs in a linear fashion. The most obvious alternative is to assume geometric or exponential population growth. In order to ascertain whether or not differing population growth assumptions would have an important effect on the conclusions of this study which are obtained through decomposition procedures and projection procedures, an alternative set of population estimates were derived through interpolation and extrapolation, as described above, but assuming exponential change. These new population estimates then were employed to derive new decompositions and new projections with the procedures described in the text and the appendix. The results for every country are similar to the ones founded upon the linear population estimates.

## COUNTRIES INCLUDED IN CROSS-NATIONAL ESTIMATES

The 83 countries included in the new cross-national analyses presented in Chapter 9 are: Afghanistan, Algeria, Angola, Bolivia, Brazil, Burundi, Cameroon, Central African Republic, Chad, Chile, Colombia, Congo, Costa Rica, Cuba, Dahomey/Benin, Dominican Republic, Ecuador, Egypt, El Salvador, Ethiopia, Fiji, Ghana, Guatemala, Guinea, Haiti, Honduras, Hong Kong, India, Indonesia, Iran, Iraq, Ivory Coast, Jamaica, Jordan, Kenya, South Korea, Kuwait, Laos, Lebanon, Lesotho, Liberia, Libyan Arab Republic, Madagascar, Malawi, Malaysia, Mali, Mauritania, Mauritius, Mexico, Mongolia, Morocco, Mozambique, Nepal, Nicaragua, Niger, Nigeria, Pakistan, Panama, Papua New Guinea, Paraguay, Peru, Philippines, Rwanda, Saudi Arabia, Senegal, Sierra Leone, Singapore, Somalia, Sri Lanka, Sudan, Syrian Arab Republic, Tanzania, Thailand, Togo, Trinidad and Tobago, Tunisia, Turkey, Uganda, Upper Volta, Yemen, P.D.R. of Yemen, Zaire, and Zambia.

# Bibliography

Aird, J. 1982. Population Studies and Population Policy in China. Population and Development Review 8: 267–297.

Alker, H.W. Jr. 1969. A Typology of Ecological Fallacies. Pp. 69–86 in M. Dogan and S. Rokkan (eds.), Quantitative Ecological Analysis in the Social Sciences. Cambridge, Mass.: MIT Press.

Alwin, D.F., and R.M. Hauser. 1975. The Decomposition of Effects in Path Analysis. American Sociological Review 40: 37–47.

Anderson, J.E., M.C.E. Cheng, and F.K. Wan. 1977. A Component Analysis of Recent Fertility Decline in Singapore. Studies in Family Planning 8: 282–287.

Balakrishnan, T.R. 1973. A Cost Benefit Analysis of the Barbados Family Planning Programme. Population Studies 27: 353–364.

Barclay, G.W. 1954. Colonial Development and Population in Taiwan. Princeton: Princeton University Press.

Bean, L.L., and W. Seltzer. 1968. Couple Years of Protection and Births Prevented: A Methodological Examination. Demography 5: 947–959.

Benedict, B. 1958. Education Without Opportunity: Education, Economics, and Communalism in Mauritius. Human Relations 11: 315–329.

———. 1965. Mauritius: Problems of a Plural Society. New York: Frederick A. Praeger, Publishers.

Berelson, B. 1963. Communication, Communication Research, and Family Planning. Pp. 159–171 in Emerging Techniques in Population Research, Proceedings of the Thirty-ninth Annual Conference of the Milbank Memorial Fund. New York: Milbank Memorial Fund.

———, and R. Freedman. 1964. A Study in Fertility Control. Scientific American 210: 29–38.

Blake, J. 1965. Demographic Science and the Redirection of Population Policy. Pp. 41–69 in M.C. Sheps and J.C. Ridley (eds.), Public Health and Population Change. Pittsburgh: University of Pittsburgh Press.

———. 1973. Fertility Control and the Problem of Voluntarism. Pp. 279–283 in Scientists and World Affairs (Proceedings of the Twenty-second Pugwash Conference on Science and World Affairs, September 7–12). London.

————, and P. Das Gupta. 1975. Reproductive Motivation Versus Contraceptive Technology: Is Recent American Experience an Exception? Population and Development Review 1: 229–249.

Bogue, D.J. 1967. The End of the Population Explosion. The Public Interest 7: 11–20.

————, and A.O. Tsui. 1979a. Zero World Population Growth? The Public Interest 55: 99–113.

————, and A.O. Tsui. 1979b. A Reply to Paul Demeny's "On the End of the Population Explosion." Population and Development Review 5: 479–494.

Bohrnstedt, G.W. 1969. Observations on the Measurement of Change. Pp. 113–133 in E.F. Borgatta (ed.), Sociological Methodology: 1969. San Francisco: Jossey-Bass, Inc.

Brookfield, H.C. 1957. Mauritius: Demographic Upsurge and Prospect. Population Studies 11: 102–122.

Bumpass, L., and C.F. Westoff. 1970. The "Perfect Contraceptive" Population. Science 169: 1177–1182.

Campbell, D.T. 1969. Reforms as Experiments. American Psychologist 24: 409–429.

————, and A. Erlebacher. 1970a. How Regression Artifacts in Quasi-Experimental Evaluations Can Mistakenly Make Compensatory Education Look Harmful. Pp. 185–210 in J. Hellmuth (ed.), Disadvantaged Child, Vol. 3. New York: Brunner/Mazel, Inc.

————. 1970b. Reply to Replies. Pp. 221–225 in J. Hellmuth (ed.) Disadvantaged Child, Vol. 3. New York: Brunner/Mazel, Inc.

————, and J.C. Stanley. 1963. Experimental and Quasi-Experimental Designs for Research. Chicago: Rand McNally & Co.

Carmines, E.G., and R.A. Zeller, 1979. Reliability and Validity. Beverly Hills: Sage Publications.

Chandrasekaran, C., and A.I. Hermalin (eds.). 1975. Measuring the Effect of Family Planning Programs on Fertility. Dolhain, Belgium: Ordina Editions for the International Union for the Scientific Study of Population, Development Centre of the Organization for Economic Co-operation and Development.

Chang, C.T., and P.M. Hauser. 1975. The Impact on Fertility of Singapore's Family Planning Program. Pp. 381–425 in C. Chandrasekaran and A.I. Hermalin (eds.), Measuring the Effect of Family Planning Programs on Fertility. Dolhain, Belgium: Ordina Editions for the International Union for the Scientific Study of Population, Development Centre of the Organization for Economic Co-operation and Development.

Chang, Y. 1966. The Economically Active Population. Pp. 181–233 in Y. Chang, H.Y. Lee, E. Yu, and T.H. Kwon (eds.), A Study of the Korean Population: 1966. Seoul, Korea: The Population and Development Studies Center, Seoul National University.

Chang, M.C., T.H. Liu, and L.P. Chow. 1969. Study by Matching of the Demographic Impact of an IUD Program. Milbank Memorial Fund Quarterly 22: 347–359.

Chen, P., and Kols, A. 1982. Population and Birth Planning in the People's Republic of China. Population Reports, Series J. Number 25. Baltimore: Population Information Program, The Johns Hopkins University.

Cho, L.J. 1973a. The Demographic Situation in the Republic of Korea, Paper presented at the annual meeting of the Population Association of America, New Orleans, published as Paper 29, of the East-West Population Institute, Honolulu, Hawaii.

―――. 1973b. The Own-Children Approach to Fertility Estimation: An Elaboration. Pp. 263–281 in Proceedings of the International Population Conference, Liege, 1973, Vol. 2, Liege: International Union for the Scientific Study of Population.

Chow, L.P. 1968. A Study of the Demographic Impact of an IUD Program. Population Studies 22: 347–359.

―――. 1969. Taiwan: Demographic Impact of an IUD Program. Studies in Family Planning 45: 1–6.

―――. 1970. Family Planning in Taiwan, Republic of China: Progress and Prospects. Population Studies 24: 339–352.

―――. 1974. The Island-Wide Family Planning Programme in Taiwan: Analysis of the Accomplishments of the Past Eight Years. Population Studies 28: 107–126.

Choy, B.Y. 1971. Korea: A History. Rutland, Vermont: Charles E. Tuttle Company.

Clague, A.S., and J.C. Ridley. 1974. The Assessment of Three Methods of Estimating Births Averted. Pp. 329–382 in B. Dyke and J. Walters (eds.), Computer Simulation in Human Population Studies. New York: Academic Press.

Cleland, J.G., and S. Singh. 1980. Islands and the Demographic Transition. World Development 8: 962–999.

Cochrane, S.H. 1979. Fertility and Education: What Do We Really Know? Washington, D.C.: The World Bank.

Cohen, J., and P. Cohen. 1975. Applied Multiple Regression: Correlation Analysis for the Behavioral Sciences. Hillsdale, New Jersey: Lawrence Erlbaum Associates.

Cuca, R., and C.S. Pierce. 1977. Experiments in Family Planning: Lessons from the Developing World. Baltimore: The Johns Hopkins University Press for the World Bank.

Das Gupta, P. 1978. A General Method of Decomposing a Difference Between Two Rates Into Several Components. Demography 15: 99–112.

David, H. 1982. Incentives, Reproductive Behavior, and Integrated Community Development in Asia. Studies in Family Planning 13(5): 159–173.

Davis, K. 1963. The Theory of Change and Response in Modern Demographic History. Population Index 29: 345–366.

―――. 1967. Population Policy: Will Current Programs Succeed? Science 158: 730–739.

―――. 1969. World Urbanization 1950–1970, Volume I, Basic Data for Cities, Countries, and Regions. Berkeley: Institute of International Studies, University of California.

―――. 1971. The Nature and Purpose of Population Policy. Pp. 3–29 in K. Davis and F.G. Styles (eds.), California's Twenty Million. Berkeley: In-

stitute of International Studies, University of California, Berkeley.
———. 1972. The Changing Balance of Births and Deaths. Pp. 13–33 in H. Brown and E. Hutchings, Jr. (eds.), Are Our Descendants Doomed? New York: Viking Press.
———. 1975. Asia's Cities: Problems and Options. Population and Development Review. 1: 71–86.
———, and J. Blake. 1956. Social Structure and Fertility: An Analytic Framework. Economic Development and Cultural Change. 4: 211–235.
Demeny, Paul. 1979a. On the End of the Population Explosion. Population and Development Review 5: 141–162.
———. 1979b. On the End of the Population Explosion: A Rejoinder. Population and Development Review 5: 495–504.
Demerath, N.J. 1976. Birth Control and Foreign Policy. New York: Harper and Row Publishers.
Dixon, R.B. 1978a. Rural Women at Work: Strategies for Development in South Asia. Baltimore: The Johns Hopkins University Press for Resources for the Future.
———. 1978b. On Drawing Policy Conclusions from Multiple Regressions: Some Queries and Dilemmas. Studies in Family Planning 9(10–11): 286–287.
Duncan, O.D. 1970. Partials, Partitions, and Paths. Pp. 38–47 in E.F. Borgatta (ed.), Sociological Methodology: 1970. San Francisco: Jossey-Bass, Inc.
———. 1975. Structural Equation Models. New York: Academic Press.
Edmondson, Janet C. 1981. Fertility Transition in Bali: Changing Economic Strategies and Family Planning, A Preliminary Report. Presented at the annual meeting of the Population Association of America, March 25–26, 1981.
English, B.H. 1971. Liberacion Nacional in Costa Rica. Gainesville: University of Florida Press.
Entwisle, B. 1981. CBR Versus TFR in Cross-National Fertility Research. Demography 18: 635–643.
Fawcett, J.T. and S.E. Khoo. 1980. Singapore: Rapid Fertility Transition in a Compact Society. Population and Development Review 6 (4): 549–579.
Forrest, J.D., and J.A. Ross. 1978. Fertility Effects of Family Planning Programs: A Methodological Review. Social Biology 25: 145–163.
Fox, J. 1980. Effect Analysis in Structural Equation Models. Sociological Methods and Research 9: 3–28.
Freedman, R., et al. 1969. Hong Kong: The Continuing Fertility Decline, 1967. Studies in Family Planning 44: 8–15.
———. 1970. Hong Kong's Fertility Decline, 1961–1968. Population Index 36: 3–18.
———, and A.L. Adlakha. 1968. Recent Fertility Declines in Hong Kong: The Role of the Changing Age Structure. Population Studies 22: 181–198.
———, and B. Berelson. 1976. The Record of Family Planning Programs. Studies in Family Planning 7: 1–40.
———, J.Y. Peng, J.Y. Takeshita, and T.H. Sun. 1963. Fertility Trends in Taiwan: Tradition and Change. Population Studies 16: 219–236.

————, and T.H. Sun. 1969. Taiwan: Fertility Trends in a Crucial Period of Transition. Studies in Family Planning 49: 15–19.

————, and J.Y. Takeshita. 1969. Family Planning in Taiwan. Princeton: Princeton University Press.

————, J.Y. Takeshita, and T.H. Sun. 1964. Fertility and Family Planning in Taiwan: A Case Study of the Demographic Transition. American Journal of Sociology 70: 16–27.

Godwin, R.K. 1975. A Cross-Sectional Analysis of Population Policy Determinants Using Situational Data. Pp. 75–124 in R.K. Godwin (ed.), Comparative Policy Analysis. Lexington, Mass.: Lexington Books.

Gomez, M., and V.V. Bermudez. 1974. Costa Rica. Country Profiles. New York: Population Council.

————, and J. Reynolds. 1973. Numerator Analysis of Fertility Change in Costa Rica: A Methodological Examination. Studies in Family Planning 4: 317–326.

Gordon, R.A. 1968. Issues in the Multiple Regression. American Journal of Sociology 73: 592–616.

Hauser, P.M. 1967. Family Planning and Population Programs: A Book Review Article. Demography 4: 397–414.

————. 1969. Population: More than Family Planning. Medical Education 44: 20–29.

Hermalin, A.I. 1968. Taiwan: An Area Analysis of the Effect of Acceptances on Fertility. Studies in Family Planning 33: 7–11.

Hernandez, D.J. 1975. Evaluation of the Demographic Impact of Family Planning Programs in Underdeveloped Countries: A Critique. Unpublished Manuscript.

————. 1981a. The Impact of Family Planning Programs on Fertility in Developing Countries: A Critical Evaluation. Social Science Research 10: 32–66.

————. 1981b. A Note on Measuring the Independent Impact of Family Planning Programs on Fertility Declines. Demography 18: 627–634.

————. 1984. Fertility Reduction Policies and Poverty in Third World Countries: Ethical Issues. Journal of Applied Behavioral Science 20.

————. (forthcoming). Population Policy, The Social Science Encyclopaedia. Boston: Routledge and Kegan Paul.

Hull, T.H., V.J. Hull, and M. Singarimbun. 1977. Indonesia's Family Planning Story: Success and Challenge. Population Bulletin 32 (6). Washington, D.C.: Population Reference Bureau.

Hyman, H. 1955. Survey Design and Analysis. New York: The Free Press.

Jacobsen, J. 1983. Promoting Population Stabilization: Incentives for Small Families. Worldwatch Paper 54. Washington, D.C.: Worldwatch Institute.

Johnson, J.T., B.A. Tan, and L. Corsa. 1973. Assessment of Family Planning Programme Effects on Births: Preliminary Results Obtained Through Direct Matching of Birth and Programme Records. Population Studies 27: 85–96.

Johnston, J. 1972. Econometric Methods. New York: McGraw-Hill.

Kangas, L.W. 1970. Integrated Incentives for Fertility Control. Science 169: 1278–1283.

Keeny, S.M. 1965. Korea and Taiwan: Two National Programs. Studies in Family Planning 6: 1–6.

————. 1966. Korea and Taiwan: The 1965 Story. Studies in Family Planning 10: 1–6.

King, T., et al. 1974. Appendix B, The Relationship Between Program Inputs, Socio-economic Levels, and Family Planning Performance: A Regression Analysis. Pp. 149–163 in Population Policies and Economic Development, A World Bank Staff Report. Baltimore: The Johns Hopkins University Press.

Kirk, D. 1969. Natality in the Developing Countries: Recent Trends and Prospects. Pp. 75–98 in S.J. Behrman, L. Corsa, Jr., and R. Freeman (eds.), Fertility and Family Planning: A World View. Ann Arbor: The University of Michigan Press.

Kitagawa, E.M. 1955. Components of a Difference Between Two Rates. Journal of the American Statistical Association 50: 1168–1194.

Kuznets, P.W. 1977. Economic Growth and Structure in the Republic of Korea. New Haven: Yale University Press.

Kwon, T.K. 1974. Evaluation of Adequacy and Accuracy of Census Data. Pp. 1–60 in Y. Chang, H.Y. Lee, E.Y. Yu, and T.H. Kwon (eds.), A Study of the Korean Population, 1966. Seoul, Korea: The Population and Development Studies Center, Seoul National University.

————, H.Y. Lee, Y. Chang, and E.Y. Yu. 1975. The Population of Korea. Seoul, Korea: The Population and Development Studies Center, Seoul National University.

Lee, B.M., and J. Isbister. 1966. The Impact of Birth Control Programs on Fertility. Pp. 737–758 in B. Berelson et al. (eds.), Family Planning and Population Programs. Chicago: University of Chicago.

Lewison, D. 1983. Sources of Population and Family Planning Assistance. Population Reports XI (No. 26), Series J. Baltimore: Population Information Program, The Johns Hopkins University.

Li, W.L. 1973. Temporal and Spatial Analysis of Fertility Decline in Taiwan. Population Studies 27: 97–104.

Lightborne, R., and S. Singh. 1982. The World Fertility Survey: Charting Global Childbearing. Population Bulletin 37 (1). Washington, D.C.: Population Reference Bureau.

Loether, H.J., and D.G. McTavish. 1976. Descriptive and Inferential Statistics. Boston: Allyn and Bacon, Inc.

Mamdani, M. 1972. The Myth of Population Control. New York: Monthly Review Press.

Mauldin, W.P. 1967. Measurement and Evaluation of National Family Planning Programs. Demography 4: 71–80.

————. 1968. Births Averted by Family Planning Programs. Studies in Family Planning 33: 1–7.

————, and B. Berelson. 1978a. Conditions of Fertility Decline in Developing Countries, 1965–75. Studies in Family Planning 9: 89–147.

————. 1978b. Reply. Studies in Family Planning 9: 288.

Mauritius, Central Statistical Office. 1953. Census 1952 of Mauritius and of Its Dependencies, Part I. Port Louis, Mauritius: H.F. Kelly, Acting Government Printer.

――――. 1962. 1962 Population Census of Mauritius and Its Dependencies. Port Louis, Mauritius: Government Press.

――――. 1972. 1972 Population Census of Mauritius, Preliminary Report. Port Louis, Mauritius.

――――. 1974. Bi-Annual Digest of Statistics, 9. Port Louis, Mauritius.

McNicoll, G. 1975. Community-Level Policy: An Exploration. Population and Development Review 1: 1–21.

――――. 1978. On Fertility Research. Population and Development Review 4: 681–693.

――――. 1980. Institutional Determinants of Fertility Change. Population and Development Review 6: 441–462.

Meade, J.E., et al. 1968. The Economic and Social Structure of Mauritius. London: Frank Cass and Company Limited.

Moon, H.S., S. Han, and S. Choi. 1973. Fertility and Family Planning: An Interim Report on 1971 Fertility-Abortion Survey. Korea: Korean Institute for Family Planning.

Namboodiri, N.K., L.F. Carter, and H.M. Blalock, Jr. 1975. Applied Multivariate Analysis and Experimental Designs. New York: McGraw-Hill.

Nortman, D. 1971. Population and Family Planning Programs: A Factbook. Reports on Population/Family Planning 2 (1971 Edition). New York: Population Council.

――――. 1973. Population and Family Planning Programs: A Factbook. Reports on Population/Family Planning 2 (Fifth Edition). New York: Population Council.

――――. 1974. Population and Family Planning Programs: A Factbook. Reports on Population/Family Planning 2 (Sixth Edition). New York: Population Council.

――――. 1975a. Population and Family Planning Programs: A Factbook. Reports on Population/Family Planning 2 (Seventh Edition). New York: Population Council.

――――. 1975b. A Longitudinal Analysis of Population Policies in Developing Countries. Pp. 19–45 in R.K. Godwin (ed.), Comparative Policy Analysis. Lexington, Mass.: Lexington Books.

――――. 1982. Population and Family Planning Programs: A Compendium of Data through 1981. 11th Edition. New York: The Population Council.

Potter, Robert G., Jr. 1963. Additional Measures of Use Effectiveness in Contraception. Milbank Memorial Fund Quarterly 41: 400–418.

――――. 1966. Application of the Life Table Techniques to Measurement of Contraceptive Effectiveness. Demography 3: 297–304.

――――. 1967. The Multiple Decrement Life Table as an Approach to the Measurement of Use Effectiveness and Demographic Effectiveness of Contraception. Pp. 869–883 in Contributed Papers, Sydney Conference, International Union for the Scientific Study of Population.

――――. 1969. Estimating Births Averted in a Family Planning Program. Pp. 413–434 in S.J. Behrman, L. Corsa, Jr., and R. Freedman (eds.), Fertility and Family Planning: A World View. Ann Arbor: The University of Michigan Press.

———, R. Freedman, and L.P. Chow. 1968. Taiwan's Family Planning Program. Science 160: 848–853.

Ramdin, T. 1969. Mauritius: A Geographical Survey. London: University of Tutorial Press Ltd.

Ravenholt, R.T., and J. Chao. 1974a. Availability of Family Planning Services the Key to Rapid Fertility Reduction. Family Planning Perspectives 6: 217–223.

———, and J. Chao. 1974b. World Fertility Trends, 1974. Family Planning Programs, Population Report Series J. No. 2: 21–39.

Repetto, R. 1979. Economic Equality and Fertility in Developing Countries. Baltimore: Johns Hopkins University Press.

Republic of China. 1956. A Census Report of the Republic of China. Volume 2, Taiwan Province, Part 2. Age and Marital Status of the Population. September 6, 1956.

———, Ministry of the Interior. 1966. 1966 Taiwan Demographic Fact Book. Taipei, Taiwan.

———. 1973. 1973 Taiwan Demographic Fact Book. Taipei, Taiwan.

———. 1975a. 1975 Taiwan-Fukien Demographic Fact Book. Taipei, Taiwan.

———. 1975b. Directorate General of Budget, Accounting and Statistics. Executive Yuan. 1975 Statistical Yearbook of the Republic of China. Taiwan.

———. 1976. 1976 Statistical Yearbook of the Republic of China. Taiwan.

Republic of Korea. 1960. 1960 Population and Housing Census of Korea, Volume 1. Complete Tabulation Report, 11–1 Whole Country. Economic Planning Board.

———. 1966. 1966 Population Census Report of Korea, 12–1 Whole Country. Economic Planning Board.

———. 1970. 1970 Population and Housing Census Report, Volume 1, Complete Enumeration, 12–1 Republic of Korea. Economic Planning Board.

Republica de Costa Rica, Ministerio de Economia y Hacienda, Direccion General de Estadistica y Censos. 1953. Censo de Poblacion de Costa Rica (22 de Mayo de 1950). San Jose Government Printing Office.

———. 1966. 1963 Censo de Poblacion. San Jose.

———. 1974. Censo de Poblacion 1973. San Jose.

Retherford, R.D., and L.J. Cho. 1973. Comparative Analysis of Recent Fertility Trends in East Asia. Pp. 163–181 in Proceedings of the International Population Conference, Liege, 1973. Vol. 2, Liege: International Union for the Scientific Study of Population.

Reynolds, J. 1972. Evaluation of Family Planning Program Performance: A Critical Review. Demography 9: 69–86.

———. 1973. Costa Rica: Measuring the Demographic Impact of Family Planning Programs. Studies in Family Planning 4: 310–316.

Riecken, H.W., and R.F. Boruch. 1974. Social Experimentation. New York: Academic Press.

Robinson, W.S. 1950. Ecological Correlations and the Behaviour of Individuals. American Sociological Review 15: 351–357.

Ross, J.A., and J.D. Forrest. 1978. The Demographic Assessment of Family Planning Programs: A Bibliographic Essay. Population Index 44: 8–27.

Rossi, P.H., and W. Williams (eds.). 1972. Evaluating Social Programs: Theory, Practice, and Politics. New York: Seminar Press.

Saw, S.H. 1980. Population Control for Zero Growth in Singapore. Oxford: Oxford University Press.

Seltzer, W. 1970. Measurement of Accomplishment: the Evaluation of Family Planning Efforts. Studies in Family Planning 53: 9–16.

Sinding, S.W., and C.J. Hemmer. 1975. Population Policy Development: The Application of Theory. Pp. 267–282 in R.K. Godwin (ed.), Comparative Policy Analysis. Lexington, Mass.: Lexington Books.

Srikantan, K.S. 1977. The Family Planning Program in the Socioeconomic Context. New York: The Population Council.

Stolzenberg, R.M. 1979. The Measurement and Decomposition of Causal Effects in Nonlinear and Nonadditive Models. Pp. 459–488 in K.F. Schuessler (ed.), Sociological Methodology: 1980. San Francisco: Jossey-Bass.

Studies in Family Planning. 1967 (January). Declaration of Population (No. 16).

————. 1968 (January). Declaration on Population: The World Leaders Statement (No. 26).

Stycos, J.M. 1971. Ideology, Faith, and Family Planning in Latin America. New York: McGraw-Hill.

Sun, T.H. 1975. The Impact on Fertility of Taiwan's Family Planning Program. Pp. 427–504 in C. Chandrasekaran and A.I. Hermalin (eds.), Measuring the Effect of Family Planning Programs on Fertility. Dolhain, Belgium: Ordina Editions for the International Union for the Scientific Study of Population, Development Centre of the Organization for Economic Co-operation and Development.

Tabbarah, R. 1971. Toward a Theory of Demographic Development. Economic Development and Cultural Change 19: 257–276.

Takeshita, J.Y., J.Y. Peng, and P.K.C. Liu. 1964. A Study of the Effectiveness of the Prepregnancy Health Program in Taiwan. Eugenics Quarterly 11: 222–233.

Teachman, J.D., D.P. Hogan, and D.J. Bogue. 1978. A Components Method for Measuring the Impact of a Family Planning Program on Birth Rates. Demography 15: 113–129.

Tien, H.Y. 1983. China: Demographic Billionaire. Population Bulletin 38 (2). Washington, D.C.: Population Reference Bureau.

————. 1984. Induced Fertility Transition: Impact of Population Planning and Socio-economic Change in the People's Republic of China. Population Studies 38.

Titmuss, R.M., and B. Abel-Smith. 1968. Social Policies and Population Growth in Mauritius. London: Frank Cass & Co. Ltd.

Toussaint, A. 1973. Port Louis: A Tropical City. (Translated by W.E.F. Ward.) London: George Allen & Unwin Ltd.

Tsui, A.O., and D.J. Bogue. 1978. Declining World Fertility: Trends, Causes,

Implications. Population Bulletin 33 (4): 1–55. Washington, D.C.: Population Reference Bureau.

United Nations. 1966. Demographic Yearbook 1965. New York: Department of Economic and Social Affairs, Statistical Office.

———. 1970. Demographic Yearbook 1969. New York: Department of Economic and Social Affairs, Statistical Office.

———. 1976a. Demographic Yearbook 1975. New York: Department of Economic and Social Affairs, Statistical Office.

———. 1976b. World Energy Supplies 1950–1974. (Statistical Papers, Series J, No. 19.) New York: Department of Economic and Social Affairs, Statistical Office.

———. 1978. Methods of Measuring the Impact of Family Planning Programmes on Fertility, Problems and Issues. Population Studies No. 61. New York: Department of Economic and Social Affairs.

———. 1979a. Review and Appraisal of the World Population Plan of Action, Population Studies No. 71. New York: Department of International Economic and Social Affairs.

———. 1979b. The Methodology of Measuring the Impact of Family Planning Programmes on Fertility Population Studies, No. 66. New York: Department of International Economic and Social Affairs.

———. 1981. World Population Prospects as Assessed in 1980, Population Studies No. 78. New York: Department of International Economic and Social Affairs.

———. 1982. Evaluation of the Impact of Family Planning Programmes on Fertility: Sources of Variance. New York: Department of International Economic and Social Affairs.

U.S. National Center for Health Statistics. 1977. Vital Statistics of the United States, 1973, Volume I—Natality. Washington, D.C.: U.S. Government Printing Office.

Wat, S.Y., and R.W. Hodge. 1972. Social and Economic Factors in Hong Kong's Fertility Decline. Population Studies 26: 455–465.

Watson, W.B. 1973. The Urban Transformation of Korea: 1955–1970. Bulletin of the Population and Development Studies Center 2: 55–61. Seoul, Korea: The Population and Development Studies Center, Seoul National University.

Wells, H.B. 1975. Matching Studies. Pp. 215–244 in C. Chandrasekaran and A.I. Hermalin (eds.) Measuring the Effect of Family Planning Programs on Fertility. Dolhain, Belgium: Ordina Editions for the International Union for the Scientific Study of Population, Development Centre of the Organization for Economic Co-operation and Development.

Wilkie, J.W. 1976. Statistical Abstract of Latin America, Volume 17 (1976). Los Angeles: UCLA Latin American Center Publications, University of California.

Wishik, S.M. 1967. Designs for Family Planning Programs and Research in Developing Countries. American Journal of Public Health 57: 15–21.

———. 1970. Indexes for Measurement of Amount of Contraceptive Practice.

Background Paper for the Evaluation Conference (of the Ford Foundation), Rome (April): Mimeo.

Wolfers, D. 1968. An Evaluation Criterion for a National Family Planning Program. American Journal of Public Health 58: 1447–1451.

―――. 1969. The Demographic Effects of a Contraceptive Program. Population Studies 23: 111–140.

―――. 1970. The Singapore Family Planning Program: Further Evaluation Data. American Journal of Public Health 60: 2354–2360.

―――. 1975. Births Averted. Pp. 163–214 in C. Chandrasekaran and A.I. Hermalin (eds.), Measuring the Effect of Family Planning Programs on Fertility. Dolhain, Belgium: Ordina Editions for the International Union for the Scientific Study of Population, Development Centre of the Organization for Economic Co-operation and Development.

Wright, C. 1974. Mauritius. Harrisburg, Pa.: Stackpole Books.

Xenos, C. 1970. Mauritius. Country Profiles. New York: Population Council.

# Index

Abel-Smith, B., 87, 99
Abortion, 7, 9, 37, 92–93, 135
Achievement orientation, 7, 11, 56, 89–90, 130
Adlakha, A. L., 33–36, 41–43
Age– marital-status specific fertility rate effect, 48–51, 129–31; Costa Rica, 82; Mauritius, 92; South Korea, 73; Taiwan, 63
Age-sex composition effect, 13, 48–51, 115–16, 129–32; Costa Rica, 80–82; Mauritius, 90–92; South Korea, 71–73; Taiwan, 62–63
Alker, H. W., Jr., 109
Alwin, D. F., 104
Amenorrhea, 28
Anderson, J. E., 6, 36–39
Australia, 5

Balakrishnan, T. R., 28–29, 31, 41–43
Bali, 6, 7, 9, 10, 15, 137
Barbados, 28–29, 31, 41–43
Barclay, G. W., 68
Bean, L. L., 32, 34–35, 41–43
Belgium, 5
Benedict, E., 89–90, 99
Berelson, B., 15, 20–24, 41–43, 56, 100, 107, 109–18, 123–24
Bermudez, V. V., 78, 80
Birth control, practice of. *See* Abortion; Contraceptives; Sterilization
Birth order, 6
Births, illegitimate, 62–63, 72–73

Blake, J., 9, 11–12, 15
Blalock, H. M., 104–9
Bogue, D. J., 15, 20–21, 23–24, 41–43, 100, 108, 110–18, 123–24
Bohrnstedt, G. W., 108, 109
Boruch, R. F., 44–45
Brookfield, H. C., 87, 90
Bumpass, L., 15

Campbell, D. T., 44–45
Canada, 5
Carmines, E. G., 104
Carter, L. F., 104, 109
Census data, 63. *See also under names of specific countries*
Chandrasekaran, C., 100
Chang, C. T., 15, 20–22, 30, 36–39, 41–44, 128
Chang, Y., 70
Chao, J., 13, 15, 20–22, 41–43
Cheng, M. C. E., 6, 36–39
Child care, 11–12
China, 6, 7, 15, 137
Cho, L. J., 50, 72–77, 97
Chow, L. P., 15, 20–22, 30–32, 34–35, 41–46, 61–62
Choy, B. Y., 69–70
Clague, A. S., 46
Cleland, J. G., 124
Cochrane, S. H., 9
Coefficient of determination, 106–9, 121–22
Coercion, 7–9, 135–39
Cohen, J., 108–9

## About the Author

Donald J. Hernandez is Chief of the Marriage and Family Statistics Branch of the U.S. Bureau of the Census and Senior Research Scholar at the Center for Population Research of Georgetown University. He is the author of *Child and Family Indicators* and of articles appearing in the *Journal of Applied Behavioral Science, Acta Paedologica, Demography,* and *Social Science Research.*